The
99¢ A Meal
Cookbook

by Bill and Ruth Kaysing

Introduction
by Anita Evangelista

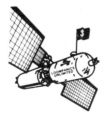

Loompanics Unlimited
Port Townsend, Washington

The 99¢ A Meal Cookbook

Published by:
Loompanics Unlimited
PO Box 1197
Port Townsend, WA 98368
Loompanics Unlimited is a division of Loompanics Enterprises, Inc.

Cover design by Shaun Hayes-Holgate

ISBN 1-55950-140-5
Library of Congress Card Catalog 96-76208

Contents

Grains

Vegetables

Nuts And Seeds

Corn And Beans

Eggs, Milk, And Cheese

Fish And Fowl

Herbs, Sauces And Salad Dressings

Fruits And Sweets

Foreword

We have been a writing team for more than 25 years. Our specialty is alternatives... what you can do in lieu of the corporate imperatives.

To enjoy good food while spending just 99¢ a meal is admittedly more of a challenge in 1996 that it was when this book and its predecessor (*Eat Well for 99¢ a Meal*) were first published in the mid-seventies.

However, as you will see, it is far from impossible simply because *most of the world's population spends less than 50¢ a day.* Furthermore, they often enjoy better health because their food is natural while much of our processed foods are worthless and/or harmful.

The pages which follow will describe how to make the best of the healthiest ingredients obtainable. You'll learn how to bake your own bread from whole-grain wheat you grind in your kitchen. There are recipes for tasty soups made from garden-fresh veggies. While our orientation is mainly vegetarian, there are delicious dishes featuring fish and poultry. Unique items from foreign cuisine are presented, including falafels and fish kebabs. Also included are some of our inventions, including Mexipop and Ruth's almond cookies.

In short, this book will prepare you to dine the way Mother Nature intended... with joyful appreciation and at the right price.

Bill and Ruth Kaysing

Introduction
by Anita Evangelista

A funny thing happened to me after reading through this edition of Bill Kaysing's book — it gave me a new appreciation for my penny-pinching ways.

It started when a co-worker was complaining about the expense of feeding herself and her almost-teenaged son. The previous evening, they'd each bought a sandwich at a quick-mart ($2 each), a small bag of chips to share ($1.49), chocolate milk for the boy and a soda for herself ($1.25) — a total of $6.74 plus tax for only two people for *one meal*.

That same evening at my house, the two adults and two teenagers present had settled down to a delightful pasta primavera. It was made from store-bought flour, home-laid eggs, and some broccoli, zucchini, basil, tomatoes, garlic, peppers and assorted other fresh vegetables right out of the garden. We generously poured goat's-milk "parmesan" which I'd prepared the year before, and ate until we were stuffed. I estimate that with the high cost of the fancy flour we used — 36¢ a pound — the entire meal for four cost about 75¢. That works out to less than 20¢ per serving, friends. And there were plenty of leftovers.

The benefits of making things from scratch, and making do with what's on hand, go far beyond the simple economic advantages. While my co-worker might complain that she had little time to whip up a big meal, the forty minutes or so my family spent in the kitchen were used to discuss daily activities, catch up on who's doing what, and arrange the next day's schedule — it was prime-quality "family time."

Furthermore, we had a pretty good idea of what kind of food we were eating in our home — I knew how the plants had been tended, fertilized, and protected from insects, so I had confidence that we weren't going to ingest some toxin that was accidentally dumped on the tomatoes. Everything was as pristine-fresh as it could be, loaded with vitamins and minerals, and crunchy, crisp, and beautifully colored. My co-worker, on the other hand, wasn't even able to determine what substances were *in* their soggy fast food sandwiches, much less how they were raised or prepared.

The kind of economy that goes on in my home has clearly also taken place at the Bill Kaysing domicile. He's a professional penny-pincher if I ever saw one, and an excellent, creative chef as well. His recipes are practical and tasty — and *fun!* Try the Potato Volcano right away, especially if you've just dug the 'taters!

Not only will this book save you money (it will probably pay for itself the first week), it will also help you think up new ways of economizing on every meal. For instance, if I'd just used home-ground whole-wheat flour instead of that store-bought stuff, I could probably have reduced the cost of the entire dinner to less than fifty cents — how's that for economy?

Thank you, Bill Kaysing. May all your 99¢ meals be delicious adventures!

Anita Evangelista, 1996

Preface

It is one of the ironies of life in 20th- century America that the less you spend for food, the higher the quality. Food that is costly has usually been over-processed and chemicalized, and has thus been rendered lifeless and useless to the body.

For example, a TV dinner of overcooked, hormone-laden meat, limp vegetables, and hopeless starch packaged in an aluminum tray with a four-color label is as high in cost as it is low in nutritional value. Conversely, a breakfast of freshly ground whole grain (wheat, corn, oats) costs a few cents a serving and has all of the original nutrients.

Bill and Ruth Kaysing's book contains many examples of how you can save your health while you simultaneously save your money.

Alan H. Nittler, M.D.

The Practicality and Validity
of the 99¢ a Meal Concept

The average person consumes about three pounds of food per day, or about 1,000 pounds per year, more or less.

While it might be boring to some, this food requirement could be met by acquiring and preparing about 500 pounds of a grain such as wheat, corn, rye, oats, or millet. Most grains double in bulk, at the least, when they are cooked.

As this is written, whole-grain wheat is selling for less than it cost during the Great Depression in the 30s, or about 7¢ a pound in the wholesale grain markets. If you bought 500 pounds of wheat at retail or about 15¢ a pound, your basic foodstuff *for the entire year would only cost about $75, or 20¢ a day, which means about 7¢ a meal.*

So, in addition to three pounds of grain in the form of cereals, bread and such, you would have about 93¢ per meal to spend on veggies, fruits, fish, poultry and other basic foods.

This is our major point... natural foods in bulk form are still very inexpensive if you buy them in that form and prepare them yourself.

Buying At Your Price

Over the years, we've had a lot of experience in buying the best food for the lowest prices. Here are some examples. We bought a truckload of whole wheat in 100-pound sacks direct from a grain dealer in Stockton. The cost was about 8¢ a pound. In the Delta we found a potato harvester who sold us a 50 pound sack for $2. True, they were culls, but still edible. Most were OK except for harvester cuts. Peaches that were too big to pack in Fruit of the Month gifts were 20¢ a pound. Cheese in bulk was so cheap I've forgotten the price. Good, too. Apricots were 5¢ a pound; we picked a truckload! Tomatoes and casaba were free by gleaning from a picked field. Walnuts also free from an abandoned orchard. Fresh salmon, two whole ones for $5 Canadian. Plums, $1 a lug box, Idaho.

This compilation could go on for pages. Want the same bargains? Then just roam around in your RV in farming country.

Another alternative that we've tried is cooperative buying, or as it was known in the halcyon days of Berkeley, the Food Conspiracy. It's a simple, effective method of joining with a half-dozen others and buying all or most of your food from wholesale outlets. Produce is the easiest, since no paperwork is needed. Just drive to the nearest wholesale fruit and vegetable market and buy your onions in bags or apples in boxes.

Next would be grains, seeds, beans, flour and related items. Being dry and storable, you can buy lots and get the price down. And so forth through cheese, baked goods, and the many miscellaneous items related to the food business.

Operating within a co-op can be enjoyable as well as frugal. For all the details, we suggest a book titled *We Own It, Starting and Managing Co-ops, Collectives and Employee-Owned Ventures,* published by Bell Springs, PO Box 640, Laytonville, CA 95454, (707) 984-6746.

A Real Close Look At A Basic Price

When we are called upon to appear on radio or TV with our book, we are often challenged, sometimes with more than a bit of disbelief. After all, these talk-show hosts dine out at exclusive restaurants where the tab for even a modest luncheon could be $20 or more. And then along come Bill and Ruth with their 99¢-a-meal book. However, we never lack total confidence, and here is why. As we wrote this section, we called a broker and got the latest quote on wheat for a 55 pound bushel with a 5,000-bushel minimum purchase. The price on May 25th, 1995, was $3.73 per bushel or 6.78¢ per pound. We called our local grain dealer and found that 50-pound sacks of recleaned (human consumption) wheat were $7.45 each or 13.5¢ per pound, a most reasonable markup. This price would readily verify the 20¢-a-day (about 7¢ a meal) cost for grain which we gave earlier. While we are citing wheat alone, the other basic grains such as corn, oats, barley, rye and so forth, are also sold at comparably low prices. Thus, you cannot miss enjoying good food at low prices if you put grains high on your shopping list.

Health Considerations of the 99¢ a Meal Concept

In various parts of the world there are enclaves of people who enjoy good health mainly because of their reliance on pure and natural food.

The Hundred Milers
Imagine running 100 miles in a day over rough paths,going barefoot or at best with crude sandals. That would require a speed of ten miles per hour from eight to six. The Tarahumara Indians of Mexico do this regularly on a diet of corn, beans, chili peppers, tomatoes and some assorted wild plants.

Chilean Miners
These tough workers carry 80-pound sacks of ore up steep ladders all day long. Their diet is mainly corn with veggies,and fruits when available.

Africans
Most have a simple, vegetarian diet of yams, sweet potatoes, corn, millet and wild plants. They enjoy total freedom from any internal cancer. Also, they are never constipated. If you have any digestive problems, may we suggest their diet.

Living Off the Land in America
Several years ago I spent some time on Orcas Island in the San Juan Islands off the coast of Washington. Just for fun I tried living off the land. Some fishermen shared their fresh-caught salmon. I traded a little kitchen labor for cheese and bread at a nearby inn. Orcas Island features an abundance of

volunteer trees: apple, plum, pear, and many nuts. There are acres of wild blackberry vines providing tons of delicious ripe berries.

After a few weeks on this fresh, all-natural diet, my energy level at 68 was far greater than at, say, 28.

We could go on for many pages citing the benefits of food that is consumed just the way nature made it. What we suggest is to try the 99¢ a meal way of life for a couple of months and watch your physical, mental and spiritual health improve significantly.

How This Book Can Help You

This book is a sequel to *Eat Well For 99¢ A Meal*. Many of the ideas in the earlier book have been expanded upon, and more important, there are many more recipes. The chief aim remains the same: to help you get high nutritional value from the food you eat at a low cost — in fact, at only 99¢ a meal per person.

Now, that may sound difficult in these high-priced times, and in a way it is. If you have typical American eating patterns, it will require you to change your entire way of life regarding food. But once you do, you'll find that your 99¢ a meal diet will just naturally fall into place. What are the changes we have in mind? To explain, we must examine the present situation.

If we were to rate the processed foods in a conventional American supermarket according to their nutritional benefits, most would come out with a minus figure: not only do they have little or no nutritional value, but they actually harm our health. Because of overprocessing and the addition of harmful chemicals, they have become devitalized and full of toxic materials. As if this isn't bad enough, due to the cost of all the overprocessing, overpackaging, and heavy advertising, they are also overpriced.

Sidney Margolius gives some wonderful examples of the bizarre economics of processed foods in his excellent book *The Innocent Consumer vs. The Exploiters*:

- The sugar in a box of presweetened cornflakes is being sold to the consumer at $4.04 a pound.
- In a box of powdered instant breakfast drink costing $3.99, the main ingredient is $1.93 worth of skim milk powder.
- Cheeses may cost as much as 40¢ a pound more just because they're sliced and wrapped in plastic.
- Dehydrated mashed potatoes cost twice as much as fresh potatoes cooked and mashed at home, but they have 50 percent less vitamin C.
- Supermarket shelves are loaded with "balloon bread" — a one-pound loaf baked in a $1^1/2$-pound pan so that it will expand to a larger size.
- A package of frozen chopped broccoli may cost only 67¢, and a package of frozen chopped broccoli au gratin, $1.19. The difference is only a few cents' worth of cheese, but the manufacturer has doubled the price.
- Those freeze-dried chives selling at $4.09 for $1/4$ ounce are really selling at $261.76 a pound, compared to a price of $20.49 a pound at a natural-food store.

But, you may say, processed foods are so convenient! They save so much time! The question is, how much time are you really saving, and for how much money?

It really is worthwhile to process your own foods. What we're suggesting throughout this book is that you grow or gather your own foods as much as you can, buy nothing but natural, basic foods, in bulk quantities whenever possible, and prepare them yourself. Here are just a few of the advantages:

- You save money... lots of it. To give still another example, a hot breakfast cereal made of home-ground, home-cooked whole-grain wheat can cost as little as 6¢ a bowl,

compared to more than 27¢ a bowl for heavily sugared, processed, packaged cold cereals.
- You get better nutritional value for your money.
- Your homemade food will invariably taste better than the store-bought imitation.
- By having a good supply of basic foods at home, you'll actually save time because you won't have to go shopping as often.
- Your children will learn that cooking is fun and an essential part of family life. Ask yourself which is better: a silent family hovering around a television set with reheated dinners on aluminum plates, or a convivial family gathered about a steaming tureen of delicious soup that everybody helped make?
- By having a basic stock of foods on hand, you'll be prepared for shortages that could occur if some disaster cuts off your normal sources of supply. As one of Steinbeck's characters says in *Tortilla Flat*, "A couple of hundred-pound sacks of pinto beans gives you a good warm feeling."

This cookbook is organized according to basic food groups that provide good nutritional value at low cost. We have recommended only foods that are available from many sources, and in some cases we've given extra tips on getting them super-cheap. There are also many items of nutritional information to help you understand the philosophy we're working from and apply it to your own needs. Finally, and primarily, there's a good collection of favorite recipes we've gathered over the years. Every recipe is designed to be simple enough for anyone to make in a modestly equipped kitchen. (The only fancy equipment we do advise you to get is a good blender, which will quickly repay its cost many times over.) In summary, you will learn just about everything you need to know in order to eat better for less than a 99¢ a meal per person.

Cooking with basic foods means asserting your independence and recapturing the joy of discovery in the kitchen. There's a big bonus, too — good health through good food. We hope this will not be just another cookbook, but a passport to culinary and nutritional freedom for everyone who reads it.

Update on Costs

The original edition of this book described three meals which cost $1 or less. Although costs have risen considerably since the first publication in 1977, it is still not difficult to enjoy three healthful and satisfying meals for this amount and here is proof.

Breakfast: A large bowl of freshly cooked millet laced with wild honey. The latter costs more than the former. Total 12¢.

   This dish is based on the preparation of millet purchased for about 20¢ per pound. Since it absorbs water when cooked, about 5¢ worth of millet will fill a large bowl.

Lunch: A giant burrito composed of a large homemade, whole-wheat tortilla filled with chili beans, green rice (cooked with parsley, cilantro, and green onions), and hot tomato sauce (fresh tomatoes with plenty of cayenne). Fold together so it looks like a giant tamale. Incidentally, this food combination yields generous protein. Tortilla, 3¢, beans, 10¢, rice, 8¢, sauce, 7¢. Total 28¢.

We Go Into *Dinner* With a Fat 60¢ To Spend! Potatoes au Gratin, and a fresh apple. Layer sliced spuds, onions and cheese in a baking dish and cook until tender. One portion is 50¢ (potato 15¢, onions 10¢, cheese 25¢), apple 10¢. Total

60¢. For that 10¢ apple, you go through the pile and find one with a soft spot. Make an offer to the produce man. Never fails me.

In summary, it would be possible to make up hundreds, yes thousands of 99¢ a meal menus. There are still so many basic foods that are relatively inexpensive that you have a wide choice. Note that nothing above arrived in a colorful package. We put in the apple challenge to demonstrate that one needs to have a little gumption to make it all come true.

You know, when you think about it, eating for less than 99¢ a meal is really fun!

99¢ A Meal Menus

Is it really true that you can not only eat but eat well on just 99¢ a meal? Yes, indeed. The 99¢ a meal diet need not consist of birdseed, hardtack, and day-old vegetables. Here's a sample of breakfast, lunch, and dinner menus for a week that cost on the average less than 99¢ a meal per person. As you can see for yourself, they offer an appetizing variety of nutritious meals. Recipes for the dishes marked with an asterisk are given in this book.

Surprisingly, many of the items shown in the menus have not risen appreciably in price since the 70s, when the menus were prepared. This is especially true where we cite such basic commodities as grains and beans. However, the cost of most of the dishes has increased about 2 to 4 times. Hopefully, your paycheck has risen in the same proportion. If not, then you would need to consider such options as growing your own, forming a food cooperative, or gathering wild and free foods. Eating less and totally eliminating any waste would also cut back any price increases.

There is a cost benefit that is seldom considered when evaluating food expenses. That is your HEALTH. Note how many of these meals are based on fresh veggies and fruits —

guarantees of more vigor and energy and less spent for pills and doctors.

It is possible that by deducting the saving of medical expenses from your total food bill you may be enjoying life for *less* than 99¢ a meal!

First Day

Breakfast
*Corn Crunchies with milk	$ .10
*Yogurt Smoothie with apple	.10

Lunch
*Red and Green Salad	.12
*Super Bean Tacos	.11
*Broiled Bananas	.03

Dinner
Tossed green salads with *Ruth's French Dressing	.15
*Egg Bonanza Casserole	.20
*Frontier Blackberry Cobbler	.15
TOTAL	**$ .96**

Second Day

Breakfast
*Sunflower-Oat Waffles with honey	$ .15

Lunch
Tossed green salad with *French Herb Dressing	.16
*Classic Onion Soup	.10
Pumpkin Bread	.10

Dinner
*Poached White Fish in Dill Sauce	.25
*Basic Brown Rice	.07
*Crunchy Salad	.15
Fruit in season	.10
TOTAL	**$1.08**

Third Day

Breakfast
    Fresh Cherries $ .10
    *Herb Omelet   .12
Lunch
    Poor Man's Scotch Broth   .12
    *Dill Bread   .05
    Dates   .05
Dinner
    *Enchilada Beans   .15
    *Homemade Corn Chips   .05
    *Apple-Date Slaw   .12
    *Carrot Custard   .12
                      TOTAL   **$ .88**

Fourth Day

Breakfast
    Sliced oranges $ .05
    *Potato Omelet   .11
Lunch
    *Cheesy Egg Noodle Bake   .15
    Steamed zucchini   .05
    *Carob Brownies   .10
Dinner
    *One-Pot Clam Chowder   .12
    *Corn Crackers   .06
    Carrot and celery sticks   .05
    *Pumpkin Pudding   .15
                      TOTAL   **$ .84**

Fifth Day

Breakfast
 Fresh apricots $ .08
 *Boston Brown Bread with butter   .14
Lunch
 *Kitchen Garden Stew   .20
 *Oatmeal-Raisin Rolls   .10
Dinner
 *Mushroom-Spinach Salad   .15
 *Navy Bean Soup   .20
 *Apple Crisp   .15
      TOTAL   **$1.02**

Sixth Day

Breakfast
 Hot Oatmeal with bananas $ .12
 Milk, honey and almond topping   .06
Lunch
 *Island Chicken   .30
 *Chinese Pilaf   .10
 Fresh Grapes   .05
Dinner
 *Ratatweetle   .20
 French Bread   .10
 *Low-Cal Vanilla Ice Cream   .07
      TOTAL   **$1.00**

Seventh Day

Breakfast
 *Apple Flannel Cakes $ .12
 Honey and butter   .06

Lunch
 *String Bean Soup   .20
 *Onion-Caraway Bread   .10
Dinner
 *Stuffed Cabbage Rolls   .30
 *Carrot-Raisin Salad   .10
 *Yogurt-Fruit Sherbet   .12
       TOTAL **$1.00**

Grand Total: Exactly, $6.78, or an average of 97 cents a day!

Basic Foods

Here's a list of basic bulk foods that will give you the foundation for many, many low-cost meals. The total cost, calculated recently at good natural-food stores, came to about $121. To this basic larder, we would add fresh fruits, vegetables, and dairy products as available. The foods are listed roughly in the order of their importance, though we'd hate to have to get along without any of them. We've also included some notes to give you a general idea of how we use them. You'll find specific recipes in abundance in the chapters that follow.

Whole Wheat: This is the anchor of our diet. By sprouting it, we have a fresh vegetable. By cooking it whole, we have a bean substitute, and by grinding it, we can enjoy fresh cereal, breads, biscuits, and a wide variety of delicious desserts. Cost: $24 for 100 pounds.

Whole Corn: We love this stuff! It's useful in so many ways that we couldn't be without it. One of the best methods is to grind it in your blender, boil it up, and use it as a breakfast cereal, or chilled with added fruits or meats as scrapple. Cost: $15 for 50 pounds.

Alfalfa Seed: Why do we list this third? Simply because sprouted seeds can provide you with almost all the vitamins you need. Not only that, you can sprout them anytime, under almost any circumstances. Cost: $2.25 for 1 pound.

Mung Beans: Get these for the same reason: they make delicious, giant-sized sprouts even in the dead of winter. Cost: $1.78 for 2 pounds.

Non-Instant Powdered Milk: Surprise! We do use this for cooking and drinking, but we use it even more for making yogurt. With the nutritional changes that take place during this process, you gain tremendously on your investment. Powdered buttermilk is a delightful variation that's great for making pancakes and other recipes where dry milk is specified. Cost: $4.76 for 2 pounds.

Brewer's Yeast: One of the best natural sources of vitamins and minerals. Brewer's yeast can be added to drinks, pancake batter, or just eaten plain by the spoonful, if you can stand the taste: Cost: $3.23 for 1 pound.

Brown Rice: Rice is a universal food, useful in dozens of ways. Just be sure that it's brown and not white, since the latter has no real food value beyond carbohydrates. Cost: $14.50 for 50 pounds.

Soybeans: Another great staple, loaded with protein, vitamins, and iron. Cost: $8.90 for 10 pounds.

Pinto Beans: We saw these on special for just 20 cents a pound because they were split. This is no disadvantage; in fact, they'll cook faster this way. With beans and corn in the cupboard, no Mexican feels deprived. One can make countless tasty dishes from this combination. Actually, you might pay even less if you bought 50 or 100 pounds. Cost: $3.14 for 10 pounds.

Potatoes: One of the most useful foods in anyone's larder, and delicious too. The Irish lived on a potato diet for many decades and worked up enough energy to migrate to the U.S.! Cost: $1.94 for 20 pounds.

Onions: If you buy them at the right time of year and store them carefully, they'll last a long time. Added to any diet, onions spell good flavor and nutritional value. In fact, they're the basic flavoring for most peasant dishes. Cost: $2.80 for 20 pounds.

Assorted Nuts: A useful source of protein. Nuts can be used in main dishes or for healthful snacks anytime. Cost: $13.90 for 10 pounds.

Safflower Oil: We use this for cooking, frying and salad dressings. Stay with the cold-pressed oils — safflower, soy, olive and sesame are good ones. Use them sparingly, since they're expensive. Cost: $3.72 for 2 quarts.

Raisins: Raisins are expensive but provide good food value. A few added to many a recipe adds flavor and interest. Cost $1.28 for 1 pound.

Dates: If you buy the dry variety, they are often relatively cheap. Cost: $9.40 for 5 pounds.

Soy Sauce: A seasoning that's vital to the success of your Chinese dishes. Buy it in a Chinese market if possible to get the real thing at low cost. Cost: $1.14 for 1 quart.

Sea Salt: An important staple; a little goes a long way. If it's from the sea, you get the trace minerals free. Cost: 29¢ for 1 pound.

Honey: The best sweetener you can buy, and it contains more food value than any other natural sugar. Cost: $6.99 for 5 pounds.

Assorted Spices: A mixture of cumin, paprika, pepper, curry powder, and others. (We like to grow our herbs at home, or gather them wild.) Cost: $2.39 for $^1/_2$ pound.

New Look at The Naturals

Since the first edition of this book was published there has been a stunning upsurge of public interest in natural foods.

At first, these were offered from bins in hippie co-ops. When they became popular, the big supermarkets became copycats, adding a lot of bulk junk.

Today, most everything is labeled *all natural* but you don't have to believe it. The best place to buy is still a genuine bulk-food store where you can check out the quality in person.

Recently, many new sources of nutritious foods have appeared in the form of mail-order suppliers. Not practical for heavy items, they could be appropriate for herbs, spices and other lightweight food additions and supplements.

New sources of natural food have greatly increased the publication of articles and recipes on this subject. New magazines like *Eating Well* manage to combine such diverse parameters as organic ingredients, health considerations, good taste and cost.

A trend is discernible. As natural bulk foods become the in thing and people discern the health benefits, we will enjoy a return to the basics. As someone told me two decades ago, "You don't have to write these food books, Bill. In time the health nuts will be the only ones around."

The old American standbys of bacon and eggs for breakfast, a hamburger for lunch, and steak for dinner are out of sight for the 99¢ a meal diner. But don't despair! The right combinations of grains, beans, vegetables, fruits, and dairy products with a little meat now and then are healthier for you anyway.

This section will help you expand your grain-consciousness and get over the hamburger habit. Start thinking of grains instead of meat as the foundation food, and you'll discover a whole new world for healthy, low-cost, delicious eating.

GRAINS

Ways With Wheat

Wheat is a staple food for billions of people, and no wonder — it's tasty, nutritious, versatile, and cheap! As of this writing, whole-grain wheat is selling for $24 per 100 pounds. This is certainly a great bargain for such a valuable food, so invest now. If you can't store 100 pounds, share it with a neighbor or friend.

Overnight Cereal

Soak a cup of whole-grain wheat overnight in water to cover. In the morning, just barely bring it to a boil. Then add dates, nuts, raisins, honey, milk, or even a bit of cream if you feel economically daring. What a delicious cereal, with plenty of body and chewiness! Try it once, and you'll have it often. Serves 2 generously.

The TV Version

We are often challenged to prove the 99¢ per meal concept on live TV talk shows. This is what we display: Grind 4 ounces of whole-grain wheat in your blender. Add to 16 ounces of water and simmer. Two large bowls of tasty healthful cereal for about a nickel each or less!

Here are some combinations to try at dinnertime:

Tasty Tomato Wheat

1 cup whole-grain wheat, soaked overnight
3 cups thin tomato purée
1 onion, chopped
2 cloves garlic, minced
1 cup celery, chopped
$^1/_4$ cup soy sauce
1 teaspoon sea salt
1 bay leaf, crumbled
1 teaspoon basil or oregano
$^1/_2$ cup grated cheese

Simmer the whole wheat with the tomato purée until the wheat is tender, replenishing the liquid if necessary. Add all the remaining ingredients except the cheese.

Simmer until well-blended. Pour into a buttered casserole dish, cover with grated cheese, and bake uncovered at 350° for 10 or 15 minutes, or until the cheese is bubbly. Serves four.

Chili with Beans and Wheat

$2^1/_4$ cups pinto beans
7 cups boiling water
$3^1/_2$ cups cooked tomatoes
1 cup chopped onions, sautéed
$^1/_2$ cup chopped green chilies, sautéed
2 tablespoons oil
1 tablespoon honey
1 cup cooked whole-wheat

$^{1}/_{2}$ teaspoon cumin
$^{1}/_{2}$ teaspoon oregano
$^{1}/_{2}$ teaspoon basil
$^{1}/_{4}$ teaspoon garlic powder
$^{1}/_{2}$ tablespoon sea salt

Cover the beans with the water and bring them to a boil. Turn off the heat and let them stand 1 hour. Then bring them to a boil again, turn down the heat, and simmer 1 more hour or until tender. Add the remaining ingredients and simmer until thick. Serves 6-8.

1995 comment: We suggest that the wheat be coarsely ground before cooking. Or crack it in your mortar using a pestle in the Old Roman manner. Will give it classic flavor and tenderness.

Wheat Sprouts

Simply soak any desired quantity of wheat overnight in a jar, drain it, and then rinse and drain the grains twice a day until they send out leaves and roots. The resultant sprouts may be eaten plain, chopped up and added to bread dough, tossed into casseroles, or used in salad.

Alternatively, sprinkle the wheat on a damp towel and let it sprout there. When the sprouts are a couple of inches high, cut them off with scissors. For more information on sprouts of all kinds, see page 91.

Sprouts can be ground up and mixed with any liquid. One of the most highly recommended health drinks.

Homemade Bulgar

Boil a cup or two of whole-grain wheat, dry it in the sun or your oven, and grind it briefly in a blender. As an alternative to grinding it, you can toast it in a pan until it's golden brown. Then you'll have an Indian-type snack that can be carried on hikes and picnics. Children love its crunchiness, and it's far better for them than any sugar-coated cereal you could buy.

You'll find that once you start making and using bulgar you'll find new uses for it almost daily. It can be added to pancake batter, bread mixes, cookie dough, granola, soup or stew, and anything else that would benefit from more bulk and nutrition. Extra guests on the way? Then toss in a cup of bulgar!

Bulgar Pilaf

Sauté a chopped onion in 2 tablespoons of oil until tender; then add 1 cup of bulgar and cook another 10 minutes. Pour 2 cups of water or stock seasoned with salt and pepper over the bulgar and simmer 15 minutes. Herbs may be added as desired for a tastier dish. Serves 4.

Bulgar is a very handy item to have on your shelf. It cooks quickly since it has been. Bulgar is one of the prime reasons why people in Third World countries can enjoy bountiful meals and health along with it.

Some Pizza Thoughts

Pizza has been described as Italy's revenge for ill treatment by various countries. This may well be true of the commercial pizza made and sold in the U.S. Most of the ingredients are artificial or laced with weird additions. Furthermore, the price is ridiculous — often $8 to $10 for a pizza of modest size and trappings.

Making your own will be both enjoyable and an exercise in saving lots of money. Best of all, the makings will be all-natural!

Creative Pizza

You don't always have to use the customary sausage or even cheese. You can make fine pizza with just a tasty tomato sauce and such inexpensive toppings as french-fried zucchini, mushrooms, or chunks of seasoned red onion.

To start, grind 2 cups of your whole-grain wheat fairly fine and mix with another 2 cups of freshly ground corn meal. Add a touch of sea salt. Next, combine an envelope of dry yeast with $1/3$ cup oil, 1 teaspoon of honey and about 2 cups of warm water.

Blend thoroughly with a wire whisk or in your blender. Add the flour to the yeast batter and mix with vigor — this is actually the fun part when you develop your arms and your appetite simultaneously. Put the dough in a warm place and let it rise until it's double in bulk. Next, roll out the dough for your pizzas and place it on round baking sheets.

Make a good Italian tomato sauce (see page 13), varying it if you wish by adding things like hot sauce, soy sauce, miso, tamari, chilies, or lemon juice. Spread the sauce on your rolled-out pizza dough; then add chopped or whole small mushrooms, chopped vegetables of any kind, seasoned garbanzo beans, or anything else you have handy. Bake in a very hot oven — 500° — until the pizza crust is browned. Serve immediately.

This recipe will make 4 large or 8 small pizzas. Roll out all the dough and freeze any you don't need to use immediately. Store the leftover sauce in your refrigerator.

The next time you want to have pizza, just pull out your dough, add the sauce and toppings, and bake without bothering to thaw.

Some Uses of Blender-Ground Whole-Grain Wheat

- Sift it and use the larger chunks for hot cereal. Try the fresh flour in this breakfast treat:
- Blend two eggs and one cup yogurt with a half teaspoon of baking soda. Add the fresh flour until the mix is like thick cream, which it will resemble. Pour five-inch diameter cakes on a heated, buttered iron skillet. Watch carefully and flip as soon as cake holds together. Repeat. These are like small crêpes and may be finished in that manner with fruit filling.
- If you just have a small amount of fresh flour, try these in the AM. Mix one teaspoon of baking powder with one cup of flour and cut in two tablespoons of soft butter. Add enough buttermilk to make a soft dough. Knead and roll out to about one-inch thickness. Use a shot glass to form small biscuits. Bake in 450° oven until lightly browned. Serve with blueberry jam.

Empañadas are Mexican turnovers and can be made with any type of filling. First make a firmer version of the dough described above. Roll out on floured board to about $^1/_4$-inch thickness. Make 4-inch circles using cookie cutter or container with that diameter (vase or jar). Place two heaping tablespoons of filling and fold over. Seal with moistened fork and bake in hot oven (400°) until lightly browned.

Filling can be: Sweetened pumpkin, sweet potato or yam, applesauce, plum preserves, pineapple bits or fruit salad... or anything else that you would like.

The Mediterranean Way of Life

Recent studies by medical experts revealed that people who live in the Mediterranean region enjoy good health and long life despite the fact that they consume large amounts of fat. However, the fat is usually in the form of olive oil, which is far less harmful than the fats which are consumed in the U.S.

People on Crete and Sicily grow most of their own food and consume it fresh. Coarsely ground grains go into their wood-oven-baked bread. Milk and cheese are from their own backyard goats, while just-picked tomatoes provide the sauce for their spaghetti and pizza. They roam the island fields and meadows. In the evening they gather at the local restaurant for music and wine. Let's face it, it's not just the olive oil that adds years... it's the pastoral way of life.

No need to discuss the contrast with life in the pressure cooker that comprises life in much of America. Thus, if you opt for a relaxed and rural life in some remote corner, you will, no doubt, not only save a lot of money, you'll enjoy a modicum of Mediterranean well-being.

Onion-Caraway Bread

1 package active dry yeast
1 cup lukewarm water
1 cup milk
2 tablespoons butter
1 tablespoon honey
$^3/_4$ cup onion, finely chopped
$^1/_4$ cup caraway seeds
3 cups rye flour
3 cups whole-wheat flour

Dissolve the yeast in the water. Scald the milk, add the butter and honey, and cool it lukewarm. Add the yeast mixture, onion, caraway seeds, and flour. Turn the dough out on a floured board and knead it until smooth and elastic. Let it rise $1^1/_2$ hours, punch it down, knead it briefly, and shape it into 2 round loaves. Place the loaves on a greased baking sheet and let them rise again. Bake at 400° for 35 minutes. Makes 2 loaves.

Cracked-Wheat Raisin-Apple Bread

2 packages active dry yeast
$^1/_2$ cup lukewarm water
1 cup milk
3 tablespoons honey
1 tablespoon salt
1 egg, beaten
$^1/_2$ cup cracked-wheat
1 cup raisins
1 cup tart apple, chopped
3 cups whole-wheat flour
1 egg yolk
1 teaspoon milk

Dissolve the yeast in the water. Scald the milk, add the honey and salt, and cool to lukewarm. Add the yeast mixture and the beaten egg. Stir in all but a tablespoon of the cracked wheat, the raisins, the apples, and 2 cups of the flour. Knead in the remaining flour.

Let the dough rise for 1 hour. Punch it down and form it into a loaf. Put it in a buttered loaf pan and let it rise again for about 45 minutes. Beat the egg yolk with the milk and brush it on top of the loaf. Sprinkle the top with the remaining cracked wheat. Bake for 45 minutes in a 375° oven. Remove from the pan and cool on a rack. Makes one 2-pound loaf.

Pantry Pancakes

$^1/_2$ cup whole wheat flour
$^1/_2$ cup corn meal
$^1/_2$ rye flour

$^1/_4$ cup wheat germ
$^1/_4$ cup soy flour
4 eggs
$1^1/_2$ cups buttermilk or sour milk
1 teaspoon soda
$^1/_3$ cup oil
1 tablespoon honey or molasses

Blend all the ingredients well and fry on a hot greased griddle. More liquid may be added if a thinner pancake is desired. This batter may also be baked in a waffle iron. For a lighter waffle, separate the eggs, folding in the stiffly beaten egg whites last. Serves 4.

Pass the Pasta

One of the oldest and best uses of wheat is in making pasta — wheat dough that's cut into almost any shape and then dried. It's amazing to think what a wide variety of tastes and textures can result when the same basic ingredients are made into pastas of different shapes and served with different sauces.

The kind of pasta sold in a supermarket is inferior to what you will find in a natural-food store. That's because the supermarket pasta is usually made from refined durum wheat flour, while the natural-food-store pasta is almost always made from whole-wheat flour with soy flour and other healthful ingredients.

Of course, you don't have to buy your pasta ready-made. It's quite easy to make at home, even if you don't have a pasta machine. Here's the simplest recipe we know.

Basic Pasta

Mix flour, preferably whole wheat, with water to make a stiff dough. Roll out, cut into strips, and dry. That's all. It makes no difference how you dry it — in your oven, under the sun, or just sitting on your kitchen table. When it dries, it's pasta.

When you're cooking any kind of pasta, pour a few drops of oil into the boiling water first. This will help prevent sticking. Also, after you've rinsed the pasta, you may want to add a teaspoon or two of sesame oil.

Gnocchi

If you want to make fancier pasta, try this:

4 cups whole wheat-flour (extra fine)
2 eggs
1 pound ricotta cheese
$^1/_2$ cup Parmesan cheese, grated

Make a ring of flour on your breadboard and break eggs into the middle along with the cheese. Mix with your hands until blended and the dough forms a ball. Knead well. Cut into 2-inch squares and roll each into a long snake $^1/_2$-inch in diameter. Cut into $^1/_2$-inch lengths. Drop the gnocchi into a large kettle of boiling salted water and cook 20-25 minutes. Serve with an Italian tomato sauce (next recipe) and grated Parmesan cheese. Serves 6.

Italian Tomato Sauce

2 large onions, chopped
4 or 5 cloves garlic, minced
$^1/_2$ cup olive oil
basil, oregano, thyme, bay leaf
4 cups tomato purée
sea salt and pepper
1 teaspoon honey
$^1/_2$ cup mushrooms, sliced

Sauté the onions and garlic in the oil, sprinkling the herbs on top to simmer at the same time. Then add the tomato purée, salt and pepper, and honey. Sauté the mushrooms in oil separately and add them last. As with any good Italian sauce, the longer you simmer it, the better. Makes about 4 cups.

A tomato sauce like this is the classic accompaniment to spaghetti, of course. And it's always delicious. But for a welcome change, spaghetti can go with more delicate sauces too.

Spaghetti alla Toscana

1 medium cauliflower
$^1/_2$ pound soy spaghetti
2 cups Whole-Wheat Cream Sauce (see page 181)
$^1/_2$ cup cheese, grated
1 pound fresh peas, cooked
salt and pepper
2 teaspoons chives, chopped

Steam the cauliflower and the peas until tender and cook the spaghetti in boiling water. Heat the cream sauce and add cheese. Place the cauliflower in a serving dish and surround it with the peas and the spaghetti, seasoned with salt and pepper. Pour the hot cream sauce over all and top with the chives. Serves 4.

Macaroni and Cheese

$^1/_2$ pound whole wheat or soy macaroni
$^1/_2$ pound cheddar cheese, grated
2 cups Whole-Wheat Cream Sauce (see page 181)
$^2/_3$ cup milk
sea salt, paprika, pepper

$^1/_2$ cup bread crumbs
2 tablespoons butter

Boil the macaroni in plenty of water until tender. Drain. Put a layer in an oiled baking dish and add a layer of cheese, cream sauce, and milk. Season with salt, paprika, and pepper. Add a second layer in the same order. Sprinkle the bread crumbs and more paprika on top and dot with butter. Bake at 400° for about 20 minutes or until golden brown. Serves 4.

For a colorful and tasty variation, try adding a layer of chopped stewed tomatoes.

A Legend of Love

One day, hundreds of years ago, a young Chinese maiden was busy preparing her daily batch of bread dough. Becoming engrossed in conversation with an ardent Italian sailor, a member of the famous Marco Polo expedition, she forgot her task. Presently, her dough overflowed from the pan and dripped in strings that quickly dried in the sun. When he discovered what had happened, the young Italian, hoping to hide the evidence of his loved one's carelessness, gathered the strings of dried dough and took them to his ship. The ship's cook boiled them in a broth. He was pleased to find that the dish was appetizing and savory. It is said that even the great explorer himself, Marco Polo, came to enjoy this early form of pasta. Upon his return to Italy, word of a delicious new dish spread rapidly, and soon it was popular throughout the land. Thus, says the legend, was macaroni discovered.

The next recipe is simplicity itself; yet it has a flavor that's entirely unique. I defy anyone to guess that the secret ingredient is blue cheese.

Noodles with Blue Cheese

Boil 8 ounces of noodles until tender. Drain and rinse with cold water in a colander. Put 2 tablespoons of butter in a heavy skillet and melt. Add about an ounce of crumbled blue cheese, some salt and pepper, and the cooked noodles. Stir gently over low heat until the cheese is melted and thoroughly mixed with the noodles. Serve immediately. Serves 2.

You can use this same method to dress up noodles with cottage cheese or ricotta, adding grated Parmesan cheese as a topping. Or try tossing cooked, seasoned noodles with butter, minced garlic, chopped fresh basil (or another favorite herb), and grated Parmesan.

Noodle-Cheese Omelet

$3/4$ cup onions, chopped
$1/2$ cup green pepper, chopped
2 tablespoons butter or oil
6 eggs
$3/4$ cup cheese, grated
2 cups cooked whole-wheat or soy noodles
1 teaspoon sea salt

Sauté the onions and pepper in butter or oil until tender. Meanwhile, beat the eggs in a bowl and add the cheese. Fold in the noodles and salt, and then pour the egg-noodle mixture over the sautéed vegetables. Cook over medium heat until the eggs are set, about 15 to 20 minutes. Serves 6 hungry people.

One-Pot Turkey Noodle Dinner

Great for that leftover turkey!

1 medium onion, chopped
$^1/_2$ cup carrots, sliced
$^1/_2$ cup celery, sliced
2 tablespoons butter, oil, or rendered turkey fat
$2^3/_4$ cups water or stock
2 cups turkey, diced
8 ounces whole-wheat noodles
1 cup turkey gravy
1 teaspoon sea salt
$^1/_2$ teaspoon basil
pepper to taste

In a heavy skillet, sauté the onion, carrots, and celery until tender. Add the remaining ingredients, bring to a boil, reduce heat and cover. Simmer for 10 minutes or until the noodles are tender, stirring frequently. Serves 4.

Global Goodies Provide Universal Appeal

In Venice, California, there is a popular cafe frequented by movie people, tourists and natives. It's called the Rose Cafe and features lots of pasta salads. Every conceivable shape and size is blended with veggies, seafood, meats and tasty dressings. In addition, the menu features Middle Eastern delicacies such as falafels and halvah. These exotic treats appeal to globetrotters and sophisticates as well as just ordinary folks seeking a bit of variety in their daily fare.

Coming up are some recipes typical of this genre — the peasant style merging taste with economy.

Use More Millet

Long a staple in, Africa, Russia, Manchuria, Japan, southern China and India, millet is still rarely found on most American tables. Yet this remarkable birdseed-like food is well worth discovering. While most grains lack two or more of the eight amino acids essential for a complete protein, millet lacks only one, lysine. Since lysine is found in abundance in seafood, dairy products, legumes, and most vegetables, just add any one of these to millet and *voila!* You have a healthy diet.

So go to your nearest grain supplier or natural-food store, pick up a pound or two of millet, and experiment with some of the following recipes. Millet is rather bland by itself, but you can learn to combine it with a wide variety of other foods and seasonings with excellent results.

Morning Millet

Brown 1 cup of millet in a little oil and combine with 1 cup of sesame seed meal (grind your own seeds in the blender) and 5 cups of water. Cook until thick (approximately 20 minutes), pour into a pan, and chill. When cold, it can be sliced and fried in oil with a slice of jack or other cheese on top of each portion, making a great breakfast (or even lunch or dinner). Serves 4.

Savory Millet

4 cups seasoned stock
1 cup millet
2 tablespoons oil
$^1/_2$ green pepper, chopped
1 small onion, chopped
1 clove garlic, minced
3 tablespoons parsley, chopped
1 tablespoon sweet basil
dash of cayenne pepper
salt to taste

Put the stock in the top of a double boiler, set it over direct heat, and bring it to a boil. Add the millet, stir, cover, and boil a few minutes. Meanwhile, bring some water to a boil in the bottom of the double boiler. Set the top over the bottom and let the millet continue to cook gently.

In a frying pan sauté the pepper, onion, and garlic in the oil. Stir in the parsley, basil, cayenne, and salt. Then add the vegetable mixture to the millet and cook until all the liquid is absorbed and the millet is tender. Serves 4.

Millet Soufflé

4 cups boiling water
$^1/_2$ teaspoon salt
2 tablespoons oil
1 cup millet meal (ground in the blender)
4 eggs, separated
$^1/_4$ cup skim-milk powder
1 cup water
3 tablespoon chives or green onion tops, minced
1/2 teaspoon dill seeds, crushed
1 cup cheddar cheese, grated

Bring the water to a boil and add the salt and oil. Gradually add the millet, stirring constantly with a wire whisk. Place the mixture in the top of a double boiler over boiling water and cook 20 to 30 minutes. Remove from heat.

Beat the egg yolks and add the skim milk powder and water. Combine with the millet and add the chives, dill seeds, and cheese. Beat the egg whites until stiff and gently fold them into the millet mixture. Pour into an oiled 2-quart casserole and bake for 35 to 45 minutes at 350°. Serves 6.

Millet Pudding

$^1/_4$ cup millet
2 cups milk or 1 $^1/_2$ cups water and $^1/_2$ cup non-instant milk
   powder
2 eggs, beaten
4 tablespoons molasses
$^1/_4$ cup sesame seeds

Soak the millet in $^1/_2$ cup milk. Heat the rest of the milk directly over the burner in the top of a double boiler. Stir in the millet mixture, place it over boiling water, cover and cook for about 45 minutes, stirring occasionally. Remove it from the heat, and when it's cool, blend in the beaten eggs, molasses, and sesame seeds.

Cook for another 5 minutes. Serve hot or cold. Chopped up dates or raisins may also be folded in, or try it with a little fresh fruit on top. Serves 4.

Millet with Vegetables

1 cup millet
3 tablespoons oil
2 cups canned or frozen tomatoes
1 medium onion, chopped

2 cloves garlic, minced
$^1/_2$ green pepper, chopped
2 stalks celery, chopped
2 sprigs parsley, minced
$^1/_3$ cup mushrooms, sliced
1 teaspoon basil or oregano

Sauté the millet in 2 tablespoons of the oil in a heavy skillet. Drain the tomatoes and pour the juice into a measuring pitcher, adding enough stock or water to make 3 cups. Pour it over the millet, bring to a boil, cover tightly, and simmer over low heat until all the liquid is absorbed.

In the meantime pour the remaining oil into another skillet and sauté all of the vegetables until nearly tender. Add the tomato pulp and herbs, and simmer a few more minutes. Spoon the vegetable sauce on top of each serving of millet. Serves 4.

Onward With Oats

Scotland gained its freedom from England many centuries ago, and most canny Scots will attribute their fierce independence to the liberal consumption of oats. Haggis, a dish packed full of rich, nutritious oatmeal, is practically a Scottish national institution.

Interestingly, the American cereal industry also uses oat flour as the basic ingredient in many of its products. But why bother to buy them, when plain oatmeal is so cheap and delicious? As a boy, I think that a bowl of steaming oatmeal laced with cream and topped with fresh sliced peaches was my favorite breakfast. My love for it has not diminished in 70 years.

Oatmeal is basic to good eating on a low budget — not just at breakfast, but at lunch and dinner too. The recipes in this section show just a few of the many ways to use it.

First, here it is, the delicious, crunchy cereal that made the food industry wake up. Trouble is, the commercial versions are sugary and overpriced. So make your own! If you buy rolled oats in bulk, you can make up great batches of this recipe and store them in large jars with tight-fitting lids. You'll save a lot of money and have a healthier breakfast too.

Granola

$^1/_2$ cup honey
$^1/_2$ cup oil
1 teaspoon vanilla
$^1/_2$ teaspoon salt
$^1/_2$ cup sesame seeds
1 cup soy grits
$^1/_2$ cup wheat germ
2 cups unsweetened coconut
7 cups rolled oats
$^1/_2$ cup sunflower seeds

In a large cast-iron saucepan or Dutch oven, heat the honey, oil, and vanilla together. Turn off the heat and stir in the remaining ingredients with a fork in the order given. Put the skillet or Dutch oven into your oven and turn the temperature to 350°. When the granola begins to brown (in about 15 minutes), stir it every 5 to 10 minutes thereafter for a total of about 30 minutes, being sure to scrape up any that might be collecting at the bottom. Raisins and nuts can be added later and mixed in well. Cool before storing. Makes about 3 quarts.

Hearty Oatmeal Cookies

3 eggs
$^3/_4$ cup honey (you can use part molasses)
$^3/_4$ cup oil
1 teaspoon vanilla
$^1/_2$ teaspoon baking powder
$^1/_4$ cup milk
2 cups flour (use a mixture of whole-wheat, soy, bran, or wheat germ if you like)
2 cups oatmeal
1 cup chopped dried fruit (raisins, dates, prunes, apricots)

1 cup walnuts, chopped
$^1/_2$ cup sesame seeds
$^1/_2$ cup sunflower seeds

Mix the ingredients in the order given and drop by spoonfuls on a greased cookie sheet. Bake at 350° for 15 minutes or until light brown. Makes about 8 dozen!

Everyone has a recipe for oatmeal cookies like the one that comes on the box of rolled oats using 1 cup white sugar, 1 cup brown sugar, and 1 cup white flour. Once you've tried this recipe using wholesome ingredients, you'll throw your old one away. They're wonderful in your child's lunchbox, in a picnic basket, or as a snack. This is a large recipe, but they store well.

Oatmeal Croquettes

Oats for dinner!

1 cup rolled oats
$^3/_4$ cup hot water or milk
1 egg, beaten
1 large onion, chopped
1 teaspoon salt
$^1/_8$ teaspoon pepper
$^1/_4$ cup oil

Soak the oats in water or milk for about an hour. Add the rest of the ingredients and drop by spoonfuls into the hot oil in a skillet. Brown on each side, drain on paper towels, and serve as an accompaniment to any vegetable dish. Serves 4.

Barley — A Coffee Alternative

As of this writing, the price of coffee has soared beyond belief. Here's a way to continue enjoying that unique coffee flavor without having to eliminate some more nutritious item from your food budget. Roast half a pound of barley in the oven at 350° for about 30 minutes until deep brown. Mix with a pound of coffee beans. Grind it in your blender or coffee grinder as desired and brew in your favorite fashion. With coffee beans at $4 a pound and barley costing only 10 cents a pound, you have now cut the price of your coffee almost in half. And the flavor? Not bad at all... try it!

Honey Oatmeal Bread

2 cups boiling water
$^1/_2$ cup honey
2 tablespoons oil
2 teaspoons salt
1 cup rolled oats
1 cake yeast or 1 tablespoon active dry yeast
$^1/_2$ cup lukewarm water
$4^1/_2$-5 cups whole wheat flour

In a large mixing bowl, stir together the boiling water, honey, oil, salt, and oats. Let cool to lukewarm. In a small dish dissolve the yeast in the lukewarm water and add it to the first mixture. Stir in $4^1/_2$ cups flour and beat well. Cover and let rise until double in bulk. Add more flour if necessary, and knead until elastic. Shape into 2 loaves and place in 2 greased 9x5x3 inch pans. Let rise again.

For a tasty glaze, brush the tops of the loaves lightly with honey and sprinkle with uncooked oats. Bake for 40 to 50 minutes at 350°. Remove from pans and cool the loaves on a wire rack. Makes 2 loaves.

Make Your Own Snacks

Part of America's dietary culture is snacks. The money-mad munch moguls make billions by processing cheap ingredients into expensive little bites. You can beat them at this game by making your own tidbits. Here's an assortment.

Crackers: Mix a half teaspoon of baking powder with one cup of whole-wheat flour. Add oil slowly and mix until the flour becomes like a light meal. Add water to make a fairly stiff dough. Roll out on a floured board and cut into strips. Place on cookie sheet, sprinkle with coarse salt and bake until light brown in hot oven. Tasty hot but if any are left, cool and store in a tightly sealed container.

We suggest that this recipe become your basic one for homemade crackers. Try other flours like rye, buckwheat, or soy. Try baking them on both sides. Add grated cheeses, ground seeds or nuts, herbs and various seasonings and sauces. The more that you experiment, the more you'll be pleased with your audacity. And think of the money you'll save!

Helpers: These are the heavily promoted profit makers that you can generate on your own for a fraction of the fancy boxed versions. All you need is a pasta, rice, cous-cous, bulgar, and a terrific sauce. Meat is your option.

Dips: Costly in prepared form, try this humus that is our favorite. Blend a cup of cooked garbanzo beans with $^1/_8$ cup of lemon juice, $^1/_2$ teaspoon salt, fresh chopped parsley, 3 garlic cloves, $^1/_3$ cup of sesame tahini (prepared from toasted, crushed sesame seeds and water). Mix until creamy.

Rice Is Right

Did you know that more rice is eaten here on Planet Earth than any other grain? Unfortunately, much of it is polished white rice rather than natural brown rice. *Never buy white rice.* It's hardly anything more than starch, but brown rice has good nutritional value.

- It's a good source of protein, though it must be supplemented by other food to make up for a deficiency in two of the eight essential amino acids.
- It's an important source of iron, B-complex vitamins, and calcium, and at the same time it's low in fat, sodium, cholesterol, and gluten.
- Its low fiber content makes rice easy to digest.

Like other grains, rice is wonderfully versatile. One of our specialties, both at home in Santa Cruz and aboard our boat, The Flying Goose, is Chinese food, in which rice nearly always plays an important part. We also use rice in lieu of potatoes, usually as a pilaf (recipe follows). It can serve as the basis for a main dish, along with vegetables and beans or cheese. It makes a great breakfast cereal with chopped almonds, a little honey, and perhaps a splash of cream. It's also a beautiful dessert cooked with milk and sweeteners such as raisins, chopped dates, or other fruit (see the Date Rice Pudding recipe on page 212).

As this book goes to press, you can buy brown rice in bulk for just 29 cents a pound. Also, it's quick and easy to prepare. Try the method below and you'll never have gummy, sticky rice again.

Basic Brown Rice

Measure 1 cup of rinsed brown rice and 3 cups of water or stock. Pour the two into a saucepan with a tight-fitting lid. Set over low heat and cook without stirring or removing the lid for about 40 minutes. After that, check to see if the rice is tender. If not, add a little water if necessary and cook for another 5 to 10 minutes. Serves 4.

Chinese Pilaf

Here's our favorite fancy rice side dish.

2 cups raw brown rice
$^1/_4$ cup oil
tops from 2 stalks celery, chopped
1 bunch green onions, chopped
$^1/_2$ cup soy sauce
4 cups water
$^1/_4$ pound sunflower seeds
$^1/_4$ pound mushrooms, sliced.

Sauté the rice in the oil for a few minutes, stirring constantly. Add the celery, onions, soy sauce, and water, and bring to a boil. Stir and then lower heat, cover and simmer about 40 minutes, or until the rice is tender. Add the sunflower seeds and mushrooms for the last 10 minutes. Serves 8.

Sesame Vegetable Rice

2 tablespoons sesame seeds
$^1/_2$ cup onions, chopped
$^1/_2$ cup celery, sliced
$^1/_2$ cup green pepper, chopped
$^1/_2$ cup carrots, grated
1 clove garlic, minced
2 tablespoons oil
1 teaspoon of your favorite herb (sage, marjoram, rosemary, or
    thyme is recommended) or a combination of several
1 cup brown rice
2 cups stock
salt to taste

Toast the sesame seeds in a pan in a 200° oven for about 20 minutes, stirring occasionally. Sauté the vegetables and garlic in the oil for 10 minutes. Stir in the herbs. Add the brown rice and stir for a few minutes. Heat the stock to boiling, add it to the rice-vegetable mixture, and salt to taste. Add the sesame seeds to the rice. Cover and simmer about 40 minutes, or until the rice is tender. Serves 4.

Curried Rice with Peas and Carrots

1 onion, minced
3 tablespoons oil
1 cup brown rice
1-2 tablespoons curry powder
2 cups stock
sea salt and freshly ground pepper
juice of $^1/_2$ lemon
6 medium carrots, sliced
2 cups shelled peas (approximately $1^1/_2$ pounds in the shell)

Sauté the onion in oil; add the rice and curry powder and stir well. Add the stock, salt and pepper, and lemon juice, and bring to a boil. Reduce the heat and simmer about 30 minutes, or until the liquid is absorbed.

While the rice is cooking, cook the carrots until half-tender, preferably in a steamer. Then add the peas and cook another 5 minutes. On a warm platter form a ring with the rice and serve the peas and carrots in the center. Serves 4-6.

Rice Spanish Casserole

$^3/_4$ cup cooked brown rice
$^1/_2$ pound jack cheese, grated
2 eggs, beaten
2 tablespoons parsley, minced
1 tablespoon sesame seeds
salt, pepper and nutmeg to taste
1 pound fresh spinach, chopped
$^1/_4$ cup mushrooms, sliced and sautéed
2 tablespoons wheat germ
1 tablespoon melted butter

Combine rice and cheese. Mix and add the eggs, parsley, sesame seeds, and seasonings. Stir in the spinach and mushrooms. Place in an oiled casserole, top with wheat germ mixed with melted butter, and bake at 350° for 35 minutes. Serves 3.

Gussied Up Beans & Rice

Here is that basic, complete protein combination of beans and rice, gussied up a bit to make a hearty meal.

1 onion, chopped
1 clove garlic

2 tablespoons oil
2 cups cooked red beans
2 cups cooked brown rice
$^1/_2$ cup chopped parsley
1 teaspoon sea salt
$^1/_4$ cup grated cheese
1 egg
1 cup milk

Sauté the onion and garlic in the oil and blend with the beans and rice. Add the parsley, salt, and cheese. Beat the egg and milk together and add to the bean-rice mixture. Bake in a casserole for 30 minutes at 350°. Serves 4-6.

Puffy Tuna-Rice Casserole

$^1/_3$ cup vegetable oil
$^1/_4$ cup whole-wheat flour
$^1/_2$ teaspoon salt
$1^1/_2$ cups milk
3 eggs, separated
1 can tuna or $^3/_4$ cup cooked fish, flaked
2 tablespoons onion, grated
1 tablespoon lemon juice
2 cups cooked brown rice
2 slices cheese

Make a white sauce by blending the oil, flour, salt, and milk in a blender, then heating the mixture in a saucepan, stirring constantly. When thickened, beat the egg yolks, add a little sauce to them, and then add the yolks to the sauce in the pan. Cook for about 2 minutes over low heat while continuing to stir. Remove from heat and fold in tuna, onion, lemon juice, and rice. Beat the egg whites until stiff and fold them into the tuna mixture. Pour into a $1^1/_2$ quart casserole.

Cut the cheese slices in half diagonally and arrange them around the top. Set the casserole in a pan of hot water. Bake at 350° for about 40 minutes or until firm. Serves 4.

Rice Ranchero

1 quart homemade tomato soup seasoned with 1 tablespoon chili powder
$^3/4$ cup onions, finely chopped
3 cups cooked brown rice
$1^1/2$ cups homemade corn chips, crushed
$^3/4$ cup grated cheese

Mix the soup and onions, and heat until boiling. Add the rice and mix well. Pour into a 2-quart casserole. Top with crushed corn chips and cheese. Bake at 375° for 25 to 30 minutes. Serves 6.

The many pleasures of vegetables are rarely enjoyed to the fullest in the typical American diet. Everybody agrees that you have to eat your vegetables to get your vitamins, but hardly anybody considers them a treat. The trouble is, too many people just rely on those high-priced little frozen packets of peas or carrots which they routinely pull out every night come suppertime. Those peas or carrots wind up sitting there on the side of the plate, sure second-raters. The real potential of vegetable dishes never gets explored.

We hope you like to garden, and that you'll start doing some vegetable gardening, if you don't already. One of the luxuries you can really indulge in on a 99¢ a meal is a splendid variety of vegetables — especially if you grow your own. When you've gathered your own produce from your own yard, you just naturally appreciate it

more deeply, and preparing it for the table feels like a reward instead of chore.

Vegetables are just about as basic to us as grains. We want to show you that they're not only healthy and cheap, but wonderful eating.

Asparagus to Zucchini

Of course, to vegetable lovers like us, really fresh, garden-ripe vegetables are exquisite in their simplest form: cooked preferably by steaming, and dressed with a little butter, salt and pepper. We might add a little lemon or orange juice or grated rind, a hint of garlic or chives, or a favorite herb for a slightly fancier treatment.

Here's another quick way to fix vegetables that retains more of their flavor than many of the conventional methods. Melt about a tablespoon of butter or oil in a heavy frying pan. Scrub the vegetable well; do not peel. Then grate it over a medium-sized grater opening and spread it over the bottom of the pan. Cover tightly and simmer over low heat, stirring once, until tender. This method requires only a very short cooking time, thus allowing for the retention of more nutrients. Try it with broccoli, carrots, cauliflower, rutabagas, turnips, zucchini, or any other kind of squash.

Still another tip: try grating a little fresh Parmesan cheese on top of those green vegetables before serving. It makes even the lowliest weeds taste good.

Now here's a whole pack of nifty ways to fix vegetables for those who may think they're not so great. They'll find themselves coming back for more!

Sesame Asparagus

Tired of the butter, cheese, or hollandaise sauce usually served with asparagus? Try this for a change. It's tasty, and the combination of sesame seeds and bread crumbs will add valuable protein to your menu.

1 pound asparagus
3 tablespoons oil or butter
2 tablespoons sesame seeds
$^1/_2$ cup bread crumbs
salt and pepper to taste

Cut off the bottom part of the asparagus stalks as necessary to remove any tough fiber. Slice them in 2-inch lengths and sauté in oil or butter until almost tender. Toast the sesame seeds by stirring them in a frying pan over fairly high heat. Then add a little oil or butter and the bread crumbs, and stir together until well blended. Pour this mixture over the hot asparagus, season with salt and pepper, and stir gently until the asparagus is well coated with the seeds and bread crumbs. Serve immediately. Serves 4.

This does wonders for broccoli and cauliflower, too!

Broccoli with Mushroom-Tomato Sauce

1 pound broccoli
1 cup sliced mushrooms
2 medium onions, sliced thinly
4 tomatoes, chopped
3 tablespoons oil
sea salt and soy sauce

Steam the broccoli until almost tender. Sauté the mushrooms, onions, and tomatoes together in the oil and season with sea salt and soy sauce. When they are tender, add the broccoli and simmer for another 10 minutes. Serves 6.

Cabbage with Caraway Seeds

Cooked cabbage is ordinarily very bland. But add some caraway seeds and a few drops of lemon juice, and *voila!* You have a tasty companion for your main dish.

1 medium head green cabbage
4 tablespoons butter
2 teaspoons caraway seeds
juice of half a lemon

Cut the cabbage in quarters and boil for 8 minutes in salted water. Melt the butter and add the caraway seeds and lemon juice. Drain the cabbage, place it in a serving dish, and pour the sauce over it. Serves 4.

Stuffed Cabbage Rolls

A delightful vegetarian version that still has plenty of protein for a main dish.

1 head cabbage
$^1/_2$ cup cooked garbanzo beans
$^1/_2$ cup yogurt
$^3/_4$ cup cooked brown rice
2 tablespoons chopped parsley
2 tablespoons chopped chives
$^1/_2$ teaspoon crushed celery seeds
$^1/_2$ teaspoon oregano
1 tablespoon soy sauce
$^1/_3$ cup chopped celery
$^1/_3$ cup grated cheese
$^2/_3$ cup chopped mushrooms
1 teaspoon sea salt
3 fresh tomatoes, chopped

Core the cabbage and steam it over hot water for 5 minutes or until the leaves can be separated. Blend the cooked garbanzo beans and yogurt in a blender, and then place them in a mixing bowl. Add all the remaining ingredients except the tomatoes. Blend well. Stuff each cabbage leaf with a couple of tablespoonfuls of the mixture and fold over the edges, fastening with a toothpick.

Place in an oiled casserole dish, cover with the chopped tomatoes, and bake covered at 350° for about 30 minutes. Serves 4-6.

Carrot Custard

The humble carrot makes a delicious dessert.

2 cups sliced cooked carrots
2 cups milk
3 eggs
4 tablespoons honey
$^1/_4$ teaspoon nutmeg
$^1/_4$ teaspoon allspice

Whirl all ingredients in a blender and pour the mixture into oiled custard cups. Set the cups in a pan of hot water and bake at 325° for 50 minutes or until set. Serves 6.

Carrot-Potato Scallop

Carrots and potatoes make a friendly pair.

8 medium carrots
2 medium potatoes
2 tablespoons butter
2 tablespoons whole wheat flour
$1^1/_2$ cups milk made from dry milk powder
2 tablespoons minced chives
$1^1/_2$ teaspoons caraway seeds
sea salt to taste

Scrub the vegetables well and cut them into $1/8$-inch slices. Place them in alternating layers in a greased dish.

Make a cream sauce as follows: melt the butter in a pan; add the flour and stir for a few minutes over low heat; then slowly add the milk, stirring constantly. When it thickens, add the chives, caraway seeds, and salt. Pour over the potatoes and carrots, cover and bake at 375° for 30 minutes.

Remove the cover and bake 30 minutes longer until vegetables are tender. Serves 4.

Summer Corn Succotash

When the corn comes in, here's a zesty combination to try.

$2/3$ cup chopped green peppers
1 small onion, sliced
1 clove garlic, minced
1 tablespoon oil
1 cup raw corn, grated off the cob
2 medium tomatoes, chopped
$1/2$ cup celery, diced
$3/4$ cup bread crumbs
2 teaspoons sea salt
$1/2$ teaspoon paprika
1 teaspoon honey
$1/2$ teaspoon basil
pinch of cayenne
$1/2$ cup grated cheese (optional)

Sauté the green peppers, onions, and garlic in the oil. Combine the remaining ingredients with the sautéed vegetables and place them in an oiled casserole. Top with grated cheese if desired, cover, and bake at 350° for 30 minutes. Then turn the heat up to 400° and bake uncovered for another 10 minutes. Serves 6.

Corn Soufflé

3 green onions with tops, chopped
3 tablespoons butter or oil
3 tablespoons flour
1 cup milk
3 eggs, separated
1 cup grated cheese
1^1/2 cups fresh corn, cut off the cob
1 teaspoon sea salt
2 tablespoons Parmesan cheese

Sauté the onions in butter or oil. Gradually blend in the flour and then the milk. Beat the egg yolks, adding a little hot mixture to them first and then mixing all together over low heat. Add the cheese and stir constantly until it melts. Fold in the corn and salt, and let cool.

Beat the egg whites until stiff and fold them into the cooled mixture. Pour into a generously buttered 1^1/2 quart casserole or soufflé dish, and sprinkle the Parmesan cheese on top. Place in a preheated 425° oven and immediately reduce the heat to 375°. Bake for 35 minutes. Serves 4-6.

Eggplant, the Meaty Vegetable

We think that the big purply egg-shaped eggplant is one of the most under-used, unappreciated vegetables in the world today. Easy to grow and quite cheap to buy, eggplant can serve as the basis for a whole spectrum of meatlike dishes.

You can chop it like diced beef, slice it like ham, sauté it as though it were a tender lamb, or cut it in julienne strips, dip them in an egg batter, and gently cook them in oil. Fried lightly in butter with garlic and sprinkled with Parmesan cheese, eggplant is a gourmet treat you will want to enjoy often. Added to any kind of sauce, it will impart a meatlike texture and flavor.

You can even dry sliced eggplant in your oven to keep for future use, much as you might do with squash or pumpkin. Try it!

Eggplant will soak up a lot of oil when you sauté it. To avoid this problem, salt the slices liberally and let them stand in a bowl for 30 minutes. Some liquid will be drawn out by the salt, which you can save for soup stock. Pat the slices dry with a paper towel, and they're ready for the frying pan.

Baked Eggplant

1 large eggplant
olive oil
sea salt
oregano and basil to taste
2 large tomatoes
bread crumbs

Slice the eggplant into ¹/₂-inch-thick rounds and place them on a cookie sheet. Brush them with oil and bake at 400° for about 7 minutes. Turn them over, brush them with oil again, and sprinkle each slice with the sea salt and herbs. Then cover each slice with a slice of tomato and sprinkle the bread crumbs on top. Bake another 7 minutes or until tender. Serves 4-6.

Eggplant Lasagna

This recipe is a good example of the ingenious ways eggplant can be used. Fresh or dried eggplant can be added to virtually any pasta sauce as well.

1 large eggplant
olive oil
2 cups stewed tomatoes
1 cup tomato sauce

3-4 cloves garlic
2 onions, chopped
1 green pepper, chopped
$^1/_2$ teaspoon each, basil, oregano
2 bay leaves
1 pint cottage cheese
$^1/_4$ cup chopped parsley
$^1/_2$ pound jack cheese
Parmesan cheese and bread crumbs

Peel and slice the eggplant and fry it in oil until tender. Add all the remaining ingredients except the cheeses, bread crumbs, and parsley, and simmer for at least an hour or until thick. In an oiled casserole put a layer of sauce and a layer of eggplant; dot the eggplant with cottage cheese mixed with chopped parsley and cover it with small pieces of jack cheese. Continue layering in this way, putting bread crumbs and grated Parmesan on the top. Bake 1 hour at 350°. Serves 6.

Parmesan

By now you will have noticed that we use a lot of Parmesan cheese in our recipes. It's expensive, you say. Yes, and we agree. However, it can add so much flavor to ordinary items that we believe it's easily worth the cost. Just one teaspoon can make a huge serving of eggplant totally terrific. Also, shop around; we've found a chain called Trader Joe's where the quality is high, the price low.

Rattatweetle

We couldn't resist giving our own nickname to the classic Ratatouille.

1 large eggplant
1 green pepper, chopped

1 large onion, chopped
2 cloves garlic, minced
2 tablespoons olive oil
bay leaf, thyme, oregano, basil, sea salt, pepper
3-4 tomatoes, chopped
2 medium zucchini, sliced

Peel the eggplant and cut it into cubes. Parboil them for 3 minutes in boiling water. Sauté the green pepper, onion, and garlic in oil and add the herbs and seasonings. Add the eggplant, tomatoes, and zucchini, and simmer covered for 20 minutes, stirring occasionally until well blended. This can be eaten hot or cold, and is always better the second day. Serves 6-8.

This is one of the most delicious and nutritious vegetable dishes we know of. People who say they hate vegetables come back for more every time, and best of all, it fits in perfectly with the 99¢ a meal concept.

Don't hesitate to experiment with this recipe yourself. We recently encountered a version in which everything was green. The cook, Ann Johnson of Santa Barbara, California, decided she was going to try a monochromatic Ratatouille just for fun. It turned out to be the most delicious version we've ever tasted. With her permission we're going to give away the culinary secret of the century: she added some green chiles that lent just the right amount of Mexican heat to make the dish literally sing!

Marvelous Mushrooms

Too expensive? Just get yourself some mushroom spores (check any gardening magazine for ads), find a nice, cool, dark place, combine the spores with a rich bed of cool earth and manure, and hang easy. The mushrooms know exactly what to do under the right conditions.

Homegrown or store-bought, mushrooms have excellent nutritional value and few calories. Also, they usually haven't been processed in any way. Fry them in a little butter for a side dish. Pop them into the next pot of soup you make just before it's ready to take from the fire, leaving them in just long enough to warm up. Overcooking destroys their delicate flavor and some of their nutritional value. Another excellent use is in salads: just slice them and toss them with your greens and dressing.

Remember, too, that when the price is low, you can buy large quantities of mushrooms and dry them. They'll add an elegant touch to your 99¢ a meal diet.

Mushroom-Corn Bake

1 pound mushrooms, sliced
1 medium onion, chopped
1 clove garlic, chopped
1 green pepper, chopped
3 tablespoons butter or oil
salt and pepper
2 cups fresh or frozen corn, cooked
1 cup grated cheddar cheese
4 tablespoons chopped parsley
1 teaspoon ground cumin
$1/4$ cup bread crumbs

Sauté the mushrooms, onions, garlic, and green pepper in butter or oil for 5 or 10 minutes. Season with salt and pepper. Oil a casserole and put a layer of corn in the bottom. Add a layer of vegetables and a layer of cheese. Sprinkle with half of the parsley and ground cumin. Then repeat the layers. Top with bread crumbs, cover, and bake for 1 hour in a 300° oven. Uncover for the last 10 minutes to brown. Serves 4-6.

Curried Mushrooms & Rice

$^1/_2$ pound fresh mushrooms
2-3 tablespoons butter or oil
1 large onion, chopped
1 teaspoon curry powder
2 $^1/_2$ cups homemade yogurt
2 cups hot cooked brown rice
sea salt, paprika

Slice and sauté the mushrooms in butter or oil. Remove them from the pan, leaving the drippings to sauté the onion in. Cook the onion until translucent. Add the curry powder and stir in well. Add the salt and paprika to taste. Then, over low heat, stir in the yogurt and mushrooms. Place the cooked rice in the bottom of a casserole and spoon the curried mushroom-yogurt mixture over the top. Bake at 350° for 20 minutes. Serves 4.

Potatoes Are for Baking

Whenever we bake something, we fill the nooks and crannies of the oven with potatoes. We enjoy some of the baked spuds hot and store the rest in the refrigerator. They keep for a week or more and are always ready to use in a great variety of low-cost, nutritious dishes. Incidentally, as a topping for baked potatoes, use yogurt mixed with chopped green onions in lieu of the costlier sour cream and less commonly available chives.

Topping Potatoes

Butter is the standard addition to a baked spud. But try this alternative. Add minced garlic to 4 ounces of quality olive oil and age for a few days.

Sprinkle the oil over a freshly baked potato and mix lightly.

Oven French Fries

Things fried in hot oil or fat aren't supposed to be good for us, so if you crave French fries, try this oven method.

4 medium potatoes
$^1/_4$ cup melted butter
sea salt, paprika
$^1/_4$ cup grated Parmesan cheese

Pare the potatoes and cut them into strips. Soak them in cold water for 30 minutes. Drain and dry well. Place them on a well-greased cookie sheet and brush with melted butter. Sprinkle salt and paprika over them and bake in a 450° oven for 25 to 30 minutes. Sprinkle with the Parmesan cheese when you take them out of the oven. Serves 4.

Potato Volcano with Cheese

Here's a recipe you might want to prepare as a conversation piece for guests. It's not only fun but nutritious.

3 cups mashed potatoes
$^1/_3$ cup melted butter
2 egg yolks
4 tablespoons grated cheese
sea salt, paprika
$^1/_2$ cup bread crumbs

Shape the potatoes into a large mound in a greased baking dish, making a hollow at the top of the depth of a teacup. Pour part of the melted butter mixed with the egg yolks, cheese, and seasonings into this hollow. Reserve about 2 tablespoons of butter to drizzle around the outside of the mound. Coat the mound with bread crumbs. Brown in the oven at 350° for about 15 minutes. Individual volcanoes for each guest could also be made. Serves 4-6.

Potato Pancakes

No section of potato recipes would be complete without a recipe for potato pancakes, the kind that begins with raw grated potatoes.

4 large potatoes
1 small onion
$^1/_2$ cup milk
1 teaspoon salt
1 egg, beaten
2 tablespoons whole-wheat flour
oil for frying
salt, paprika, pepper
favorite herbs (optional)

Scrub the potatoes well and grate them along with the onion into the milk. Add the remaining ingredients and drop by tablespoons into a skillet with hot oil (safflower does fine). Season well with salt, paprika, pepper and maybe a sprinkling of your favorite herbs. Serves 6.

Pursuing Pumpkins

Right after Halloween in many farming regions tons of unsold pumpkins are left lying in the fields, obviously abandoned. On a trip to San Francisco one day, we spotted such a field near the coast north of Santa Cruz. Bill stopped the car and headed down a slope. He was gone a long time. When he finally reappeared, I was astonished to see him rolling an enormous blue-ribbon pumpkin along the ground, bigger than any pumpkin I had ever seen before. Naturally I proceeded to chew him out, protesting that this monster (1) wouldn't fit in our VW; (2) would be impossible to store anywhere; and (3) would be too tough to even cut, let alone eat.

Not only did I eat my words, I ate some mighty fine pumpkin as well. Bill stuck it into the back seat, where it looked like Humpty Dumpty in an orange jumpsuit. Back home, he hacked it into cookable-sized chunks. I steamed them three or four at a time, for 25 minutes a batch, until I had at least 15 to 20 cups. It was every bit as tender and tasty as any little pumpkin I'd ever eaten. We ate some of it hot with butter and salt for dinner. I baked two loaves of pumpkin bread the following day, and the rest went into separate plastic bags in the freezer for use all winter long.

Never say no to a pumpkin, no matter what size — it's a bargain! — R. Kaysing

Pumpkin Bread

$^3/_4$ cup honey
$1^1/_2$ cups cooked pumpkin
$^1/_2$ cup oil
2 eggs
2 cups sifted whole-wheat pastry flour (extra-fine grind)
$^1/_4$ cup wheat germ
$^1/_4$ cup nonfat dry milk powder
1 teaspoon baking soda
1 teaspoon cinnamon
1 teaspoon ginger
1 cup raisins
$^1/_2$ cup chopped nuts

Combine the honey, pumpkin, oil, and eggs in a blender, and whirl a few minutes. Pour into a mixing bowl and fold in the sifted flour, wheat germ, dry milk powder, soda and spices. Add the raisins and nuts last. Pour into a 9x5x3 inch loaf pan and bake at 350° for 65-75 minutes. Makes 1 loaf.

Pumpkin-Cheese Pie

$1^1/2$ cups cooked pumpkin
$1^1/2$ cups cottage cheese
$1/2$ cup honey
$1/4$ cup orange juice
1 teaspoon grated orange rind
3 eggs
1 teaspoon cinnamon
$1/2$ teaspoon each ginger, allspice and cloves

Whirl all ingredients in a blender and pour them into a whole-wheat pie crust. Bake at 350° for 1 hour. Makes 1 pie.

Pumpkin Pudding

$1^1/2$ cups pureed cooked pumpkin
$1^1/2$ cups milk made with dry milk powder
2 tablespoons honey
2 tablespoons molasses
2 eggs, beaten
1 teaspoon each cinnamon and allspice
$1/2$ teaspoon ginger

Combine all ingredients in a mixer or blender and beat until thoroughly mixed. Pour into a buttered $1^1/2$-quart casserole and bake at 325° for 1 hour. Serves 6-8.

Acorn Squash Dinner

1 large acorn squash
1 onion, chopped
$1/3$ cup green pepper, chopped
1 tablespoon oil

1 cup brown rice, cooked
1 tablespoon soy sauce
sea salt and pepper
1 tablespoon chopped parsley
$^2/_3$ cup grated cheese

Cut the squash in half and remove the seeds. Set the two halves upside down in a small amount of water in a flat baking pan, and bake at 325° for about 45 minutes.

Meanwhile, sauté the onion and green pepper in the oil and mix them with the cooked brown rice, soy sauce, and salt and pepper. Mound the rice mixture in the center of the squash, sprinkle with parsley, and top with grated cheese. Melt the cheese slowly in a warm oven. Serves 4.

Summer Squash Patties

We like to use the green scalloped summer squash in this recipe.

1 pound summer squash
2 eggs, beaten
$^1/_2$ cup bread crumbs
1 onion, minced
1 teaspoon salt
pinch of nutmeg and cayenne

Scrub the squash well and chop it up finely. Mix it with the beaten eggs, bread crumbs, onion, and seasonings. Form into patties and sauté in hot oil 6 to 8 minutes, turning once. Serves 4-6.

Summer Squash Casserole

You can use any variety of squash from your summer garden — green scalloped, yellow crookneck, or zucchini — or a combination for this extra nutritious dish.

$^3/_4$ cup brown rice
sea salt, paprika
1 cup yogurt
$^1/_8$ cup oil
$^1/_4$ cup grated cheese
1 egg, beaten
2 tablespoons chopped chives or green onions
2 tablespoons toasted sesame seeds
3 cups squash, cut in chunks
$^1/_4$ cup bread crumbs

Cook the rice in about $2^1/_2$ cups of boiling water with salt and paprika. Mix the yogurt, oil and grated cheese with more salt in a saucepan and stir over low heat until the cheese melts. Cool slightly and stir in the beaten egg and chives.

Mix the rice and sesame seeds together and spread them on the bottom of a greased baking dish. Cover with squash, and pour the yogurt mixture over. Top with bread crumbs and bake at 375° for 45 minutes or until squash is tender. Serves 6.

Herbed String Beans

2 pounds string beans
2 tablespoons oil
1 onion, chopped
1 clove garlic, minced
1 tablespoon green pepper, minced
1 tomato, chopped
1 tablespoon celery, chopped
1 tablespoon parsley, minced
1 teaspoon, fresh basil, minced

Cook the string beans in a steamer. Meanwhile, heat the oil in a frying pan, add the remaining ingredients, cover and cook for about 10 minutes over medium heat. When the string beans are tender, place them in a dish and pour the vegetable sauce over them. Serves 8.

Swiss Chard

Swiss chard is a crop that not only yields a surplus but seems to go on forever, as long as you keep picking the outside leaves. Chard makes a good substitute for spinach. Simply steam it for 10 or 15 minutes, chop it slightly, and add butter and salt. It can also be used as a salad green. And here is a tasty main dish that will help you take advantage of that prolific crop.

Swiss Chard with Potatoes
& Garbanzo Beans

1^1/2 pounds Swiss chard, leaves only
1 onion, finely chopped
1 clove garlic, minced
3 tablespoons vegetable oil
3 ripe tomatoes, chopped
sea salt and pepper
6 new potatoes or 3 large russets, cooked and diced
1 cup cooked garbanzo beans or corn kernels

Steam the chard until just tender. Sauté the onion and garlic in the oil. Add the tomatoes, salt, pepper, and simmer until thick. Add the potatoes, garbanzo beans, and chard. Toss well and serve hot. Serves 6.

Tomatoes: Pick Your Own

If tomatoes are grown commercially in your area, keep an eye out along toward harvest season for a field that's being picked. Then go over and ask the foreman if you can gather a few of those left behind. You'll get a yes 9 times out of 10 because it just isn't economical for the machines and farmworkers (who do the sorting) to go over the same rows a second time. This means that in every case almost 30 percent of the crop is left behind.

Organize a group, if you like, and you can go in with your boxes and fill them up with pounds of ripe tomatoes in just 10 or 15 minutes. We've done this on several occasions.

Stuffed Tomatoes

8 large firm tomatoes
$^1/_4$ cup chopped onion
$^1/_4$ cup chopped celery
3 tablespoons melted butter
2 cups toasted bread cubes
1 cup chopped mushrooms
$^1/_4$ cup grated Parmesan cheese

Slice the tops off the tomatoes and scoop out the centers. Place them in a greased baking dish. Brown the onion and celery in butter. Add the toasted bread cubes along with the insides of the tomatoes. Gently fold in the mushrooms and stuff the tomato shells with the mixture. Sprinkle cheese over the top and bake at 350° for 30 minutes. Serves 8.

Puree Your Own

When you have a bountiful crop of your own homegrown fresh tomatoes or can glean some after a summer harvest in a nearby field, try putting up your own.

We wash them thoroughly and then simply cut them up in quarters and run them 2 or three cupfuls at a time, along with a little water, in our blender. We pour the pureed tomatoes into glass containers or jars, leaving some room at the top for expansion, and store them in our freezer for use throughout the winter. Nothing beats a spaghetti sauce made with fresh pureed tomatoes.

Zucchini

Zucchini is another vegetable that doesn't know when to quit. Anyone who has ever grown this grateful crop will understand what a problem it can be to make use of the entire output from just a few seeds. Even if you don't have a garden, you've probably got a friend who is begging you to help out with one of those monster-sized green baseball bats. Here are a few recipes to give you some ideas.

Zucchini-Onion-Yogurt Casserole

1 pint homemade yogurt
$^1/_4$ cup chopped parsley
1 teaspoon thyme
1 teaspoon sea salt
pepper to taste
4 cups sliced zucchini
2 large onions, sliced
2 cups bread crumbs

Whirl the yogurt with the parsley and seasoning in a blender, adding a bit of milk if the mixture is too stiff. Put alternating layers of zucchini, onions, and bread crumbs in a 2-

quart casserole and cover the yogurt mixture. Bake covered at 375° for 45 minutes, uncovering during the last 10 minutes to brown. Serves 6.

Zucchini-Corn Pudding

1 onion, chopped
1 clove garlic, minced
$^1/_2$ green pepper, chopped
2 tablespoons butter or oil
1 pound zucchini, cooked and chopped fine
1 cup cooked corn, cut off the cob
$^1/_2$ cup grated cheddar cheese
3 eggs, separated
sea salt to taste

Sauté the onion, garlic, and green pepper in oil. Remove from the heat and add the zucchini, corn, cheese, and beaten egg yolks. Season with salt. Fold in the stiffly beaten egg whites. Spoon the mixture into a greased casserole and bake at 350° for 1 hour. Serves 4.

Zucchini Pickles

This is a really good way to preserve your surplus zucchini crop for later use. If you like bread-and-butter pickles, you'll love these.

2 pounds zucchini, sliced $^1/_8$-inch thick
2 medium onions, sliced
$^1/_4$ cup salt
$^1/_2$ cup honey
1 pint white vinegar
1 teaspoon celery seed
1 teaspoon mustard seed
1 teaspoon turmeric
$^1/_2$ teaspoon dry mustard

Place the sliced zucchini and onions in a pot, cover them with water, and add the salt. Stir, then let stand for 1 hour. Drain. Mix the remaining ingredients and bring them to a boil. Pour over the zucchini and onions, and let stand 1 hour. Bring to a boil and cook 3 minutes. Fill hot sterile jars and seal. Makes about 3 pints.

Food Processors

There are compact food processors which will save you an enormous amount of time. We have one called an Oskar, which performs veritable miracles. It makes cole slaw in seconds, pulverizes onions and garlic for sauces and grates carrots and spuds beautifully.

The objection to homecooking has often been the time and labor involved. However a blender, processor and juicer picked up at the flea market can turn your kitchen into a match for any competition in food preparation.

We've discovered how to make unique cereal with our Oskar. Just fill it with fresh popcorn and hit the switch. In a flash, you'll have a free-flowing, tasty and quick cold cereal that costs almost nothing.

The Soup Kitchen

Soup has been the classic answer to hard times, both for the individual and the hungry masses. One can visualize the scene where a cave man tosses hot rocks into a natural container of water and food scraps. Soon it begins to bubble and steam and fragrant aromas arise. With a primitive spoon, a sea shell perhaps, he tastes the hot soup and smiles.

Many millennia later, milling crowds of the jobless line up and receive a free bowl of hot soup at an emergency soup kitchen. The same picture is created when disaster strikes a community via earthquake or fire.

Thus, whenever your own larder is getting low, think about combining what you have to make a savory hot broth. It can add strength to the body while it bolsters the spirit.

The Basic Stock

All great chefs know that the essence of a successful soup is in the stock. This can be created very simply. Fill a pot with water and add generous amounts of fish scraps and trimmings or the backs and necks of chickens plus any available veggies such as celery, onions or carrots. Simmer and skim off the froth to clarify.

Now you are ready to make a simple but delicious soup that will confirm your confidence as a 99¢ a meal professional.

Spatzen

Here's an inexpensive addition to any soup or stew. Easy and quick to make it is an ideal way to enlarge a quantity without much cost. The name is German and means sparrow.

Beat one egg and add $1/3$ cup water, $1/2$ teaspoon salt and $3/4$ cup whole-wheat flour. Stir to make a stiff, smooth batter. Drop by teaspoons into soup or stew about ten minutes before serving.

Variation: Add chopped dry dill, oregano or rosemary to batter.

Navy Bean Soup

If you've never tried bay leaves in your soup, here's your chance to find out what a nice subtle flavor they can add.

1 cup navy beans
3 medium onions
2 carrots
2 cups chopped celery and leaves
1 clove garlic
2 tablespoons oil
2 or 3 bay leaves
sea salt and pepper to taste
3 tablespoons miso
$2/3$ cup raw brown rice

Soak the beans in water overnight; then cook them until tender. Mash them slightly with a fork. Sauté the chopped onions, carrots, celery and garlic in the oil until tender. Add the seasonings. Dissolve the miso in some of the hot stock from the cooked beans. Add the beans and liquid along with the rice to the cooked vegetables, using a large 4-quart pot. Add more water or stock to cover and simmer until the rice is cooked. Serves 6.

Borscht

Here's a family favorite.

6 beets, cut in strips
1 medium cabbage, cut in small wedges
6 fresh or canned tomatoes, finely chopped
salt and pepper to taste
1 quart beef stock
2 tablespoons lemon juice or vinegar
1 teaspoon honey
$^1/_2$ pint sour cream or yogurt (optional)

Add the beets, cabbage, tomatoes, salt, and pepper to the stock, and simmer for 1 hour. Add the lemon juice or vinegar and honey. Serve hot with a dollop of sour cream. Serves 6.

Russian Cabbage Soup

$^1/_4$ pound bacon, cut in pieces
1 tablespoon whole-wheat flour
2 quarts stock
3 carrots, sliced
2 onions, sliced
1 cup diced turnips
1 cup diced potatoes
$^1/_4$ cup chopped celery with tops
3 tomatoes, chopped
$^1/_3$ cup minced parsley
1 head cabbage, sliced
$^1/_2$ pint sour cream or yogurt

Sauté the bacon and flour until brown. Gradually add the stock and stir until slightly thickened and blended. Then add the vegetables and simmer for about 1 hour. Serve with sour cream or yogurt. A side dish of buckwheat groats (kasha) will round out this Russian meal. Serves 8.

Cream of Carrot Soup

Here's where a blender truly justifies its purchase. There's just no way you can duplicate the velvety quality it will give to cream soups. This recipe calls for carrots, but you can substitute celery or any number of other vegetables with equally delicious results.

4 carrots, sliced
1 stalk celery, cut in pieces
1 medium onion, sliced
$1^1/2$ cups chicken stock
salt and pepper
1 tablespoon butter
1 tablespoon whole-wheat pastry flour
2 tablespoons skim-milk powder
$^1/2$ cup water

Cook the vegetables in $^1/2$ cup stock, covered, for 15 minutes. Pour into the blender and whirl, gradually adding the remaining stock. Return to the saucepan. Put the butter, flour, milk powder, and water in the blender and whirl. Add to the vegetables and stir over medium heat until the soup thickens. Serves 4.

Classic Onion Soup

"Soup of the evening, beautiful soup" — Lewis Carroll.

3 large onions, sliced
4 tablespoons butter
1 quart beef stock
salt and pepper
6 slices French bread
$^1/_2$ cup grated Parmesan cheese

Sauté the onions gently in the butter until they're translucent. Add the beef stock and seasonings, and simmer for about 20 minutes. Toast the slices of French bread and place one in each bowl, add the soup and sprinkle with Parmesan cheese. Serves 6.

Pumpkin Soup

2 cups diced raw pumpkin
2 cups stock
3 cups milk or $2^1/_4$ cups water and $^3/_4$ cup milk powder
2 tablespoons whole wheat flour
2 tablespoons vegetable oil
sea salt to taste

Cook the pumpkin in the stock until tender. Puree it in a blender, gradually adding the remaining ingredients. Pour the soup back into the pan and reheat it, being careful not to let it boil. Serves 6.

Super Soups

Here is Ruth's prize winner... potato/leek. It's so good you'll become an addict like me.

Potato/Leek Soup

Peel and slice two large potatoes. Chop three large leeks discarding tough leaves and sauté in butter. Add to 40 ounces of chicken stock and simmer until potatoes are tender. Salt to taste but forget other seasonings. The secret of this wonderful soup is the subtle flavor that the leeks provide. Almost any seasoning would overpower it. (Ruth is so smart and such a gourmet chef.)

One summer I lived in my RV not far from an elegant market. They sold lots of turkey but apparently couldn't sell the necks, which they priced very low... under 20¢ a pound as I recall. Toss about three large turkey necks in a big soup pot with some chopped onion, celery, garlic and a splash of olive oil. Add as much rice as you like. If it gets a little thick, just add more water as necessary. Simmer 'til dinner, salt to taste and serve with sourdough French bread spread with aioli, see page 185.

An Almost Free Menu

This story reminds me of a couple of occasions when tomatoes and other items provided a virtually free menu. The first incident took place in the Monterey area where lots of food is produced all year. Several homeless people were sharing my travel trailer which we moved around following the harvesting of various crops. One week we had access to at least a ton of big tomatoes, red and ripe and free for the taking from a machine-harvested field. That week we learned how many wonderful dishes could be prepared from fresh tomatoes. We squeezed them for marvelous tomato juice, stewed them with rice and herbs and made our own brand of pizza. A few days later we had all the zucchini we could eat and learned the many ways this delightful squash can be prepared. One of our favorites was a zucchini omelet with lots of basil. We found a ranch where we could buy flats of fresh eggs cheap so they were often on our menu.

Topping our good fortune was an artichoke field which the owners allowed us to glean. We ate all we could and traded some for fresh fish. The balance we either sold for cash or exchanged for other vegetables at produce stands.

This mini-adventure gave us many great meals and the repeatable experience of truly living off the land.

Ruth and I had a similar experience in the Delta while living between our boat and the trailer. Just a few yards down the levee was the home of a very generous couple. If you happened to buy some eggs or lettuce from them, they would add several huge stalks of chard and a bag of new potatoes. I often recall how we almost stopped our market trips and began living a fresh vegetable menu. One day Ruth said: "Bill, it's Wednesday and we have only spent $3 for everything!" Truly, this was a 99¢ a meal living at its best.

String Bean Soup

2 cups fresh string beans
4 cups water
2 tablespoons butter
3 tablespoons flour
1 cup milk
salt to taste
1 teaspoon fresh chervil or summer savory
1 tablespoon vinegar
$^1/_2$ pint yogurt

Cook the beans in the water until barely tender; remove them and drain, saving the liquid. Melt the butter in a large saucepan, add the flour and stir until blended, then gradually add the milk and the liquid from the beans. Cook until thickened. Add the salt, herbs, and beans. Remove from heat, stir in the vinegar, and serve with a dollop of yogurt on top. Serves 6.

Kitchen Garden Stew

This isn't really soup, but it's a close relative. You can substitute other vegetables if you wish, depending on what you've got growing in your garden.

1 cup each thinly sliced carrots, sliced fresh green beans, diced
   potatoes
$^1/_2$ cup sliced celery
2 medium tomatoes, chopped
1 yellow crookneck squash, sliced
1 zucchini, sliced
1 onion, slivered
$^1/_2$ head cauliflower
$^1/_4$ cup green and red pepper strips
1 cup beef or other stock
$^1/_3$ cup olive oil
3 cloves garlic, minced
2 teaspoons sea salt
1 bay leaf
$^1/_2$ teaspoon savory
$^1/_4$ teaspoon tarragon

Put the vegetables in a large casserole. Heat the stock and oil with the garlic, salt, and herbs, and pour the mixture over the vegetables. Cover and bake 1 hour and 15 minutes, stirring occasionally. Serves 6.

Freshness: One of the main reasons why Oriental cuisine tastes better is because the chefs insist on cooking with only the freshest and best of vegetables. Test this yourself by obtaining your next batch from a "pick-your-own" garden, or better, from your own.

Salads,
The Summer Saver

Get your greens planted early each spring, put in your tomatoes and whatever else strikes your fancy, and enjoy a fresh garden salad every day, all summer long. There's nothing more appealing in hot weather. And of course, the simple salad can easily become a whole meal if you add some protein — hard-boiled eggs, diced or grated cheese, diced cooked meat, fish or poultry — let your imagination go!

Remember to refrigerate your leafy green vegetables as soon as you bring them in from the garden or market. Exposure to light and warmth will destroy half of their C and B_2 vitamins in just one day. Keeping them sealed in plastic bags for storage is best. In winter, or if you're temporarily short on fresh vegetables, you can always rely on sprouts. See page 91. These will substantially replace the nutrients you would be getting from other fresh vegetable sources.

We'll include only a small selection of recipes in this section, since salads offer unlimited creative possibilities. Check pages 186 through 190 for some good salad dressing ideas, too.

Crunchy Salad

1 head of romaine
2 stalks of celery
1 medium red onion
1 large firm apple
1 raw beet
$^1/_2$ green pepper
1 bunch watercress
salad oil
vinegar (wine or tarragon)
salt and black pepper

Peel and chop the vegetables and apple, and break the romaine into bite-sized pieces. Toss with oil and vinegar, and season to taste with salt and pepper. Serves 6.

Diced Cucumber Salad

2 large cucumbers
$^1/_2$ green pepper, sliced
$^1/_2$ cup thinly sliced celery
2 green onions, sliced
$^1/_3$ cup apple cider vinegar
6 tablespoons sour cream or yogurt
lettuce
cherry tomatoes

Dice the cucumbers and combine them with the pepper, celery, and onions. Add the vinegar and marinate for 1 hour in the refrigerator. Just before serving, drain the vegetables and mix with sour cream or yogurt. Serve on lettuce leaves, garnished with cherry tomatoes. Serves 6.

Mushroom-Spinach Salad

2 bunches fresh spinach, thoroughly washed and patted dry
1 cup bean sprouts
$^1/_4$ pound raw mushrooms
5 ounces canned water chestnuts, sliced (optional)
1 cup oil
$^1/_3$ cup vinegar
$^1/_3$ cup catsup
1 minced onion
salt and pepper to taste

Combine the spinach, sprouts, mushrooms, and water chestnuts. Whirl the remaining ingredients in your blender to make the dressing, and toss all together. Serves 6.

Red and Green Salad

Last Christmas we tried this combination, and not only were the colors right for the occasion, but it was surprisingly tasty.

2 cups grated raw broccoli
2 cups chopped fresh tomatoes
mayonnaise
lettuce

Combine the broccoli and tomatoes with sufficient mayonnaise to moisten and serve on lettuce leaves. Serves 6.

Salad with Fresh Herbs

4 tomatoes, sliced
1 green pepper, sliced in strips
1 large cucumber, diced
1 Bermuda onion, slivered
2 stalks celery, sliced

2 tablespoons minced fresh herbs, such as tarragon, basil, mint,
  chervil or chives
lettuce leaves

Combine all ingredients and toss with Ruth's French
Dressing (See page 187). Serve on lettuce leaves. Serves 6.

Carrot-Raisin Salad

Here's an old favorite that's still just as popular as ever in
our household because it truly answers all requirements for
99¢-a-meal budgeteers: it tastes good, it's good for you, and it's
low in cost.

2 cups grated carrots
1 tablespoons lemon juice
$^1/_2$ cup raisins
$^1/_3$ cup mayonnaise
salad greens

Blend all ingredients together, chill, and serve on salad
greens. Serves 4.

Mexican Lima Bean Salad

1 cup dry lima beans
$^3/_4$ cup Ruth's French dressing
2 large tomatoes, chopped
$^1/_2$ medium cucumber, diced
5 green onions, sliced
1 large stalk celery, sliced
$^1/_2$ green pepper, chopped
$^1/_2$ teaspoon each garlic salt, oregano, basil, and cumin
lettuce leaves

Cook the beans, drain them, and marinate them in the dressing in the refrigerator until thoroughly chilled. Mix with remaining vegetables and seasonings, and serve on a bed of lettuce. Serves 6.

Gourmet Potato Salad

The trick here is to get the dressing on the potatoes while they're still warm.

10 new potatoes
$^1/_2$ cup olive oil
$^1/_3$ cup red wine vinegar
$1^1/_2$ tablespoons prepared mustard
1 tablespoon sea salt
1 tablespoon freshly ground pepper
3 hard-boiled eggs
3 tender inside stalks celery
1 dill pickle

Boil the potatoes (unpeeled if you wish) in salted water until just tender. While they're cooking, make a dressing by combining the olive oil, vinegar, mustard, salt, and pepper.

Drain the potatoes when they are done, and dice them as soon as they are cool enough to handle. Pour the dressing over them immediately. Slice the eggs, celery, and dill pickle finely, and add them to the salad. Chill thoroughly before serving. Serves 6.

Salads

When pioneers headed West they had a secret which you can use to provide fresh greens for your salads. The resolute covered-wagon group sprouted ordinary corn and ate the tender green blades. Buy a bag of ordinary whole corn at your local feed store. Soak some overnight and then keep damp on toweling. An alternative is to simply plant it in the ground with a thin covering of earth. Either way you'll soon have a miniature forest of tender green "corn salad."

Join this with a mini-garden in your window box of these:

Black-seeded Simpson. Can pick leaves as they appear.

Midget Butterhead. Perfect for window boxes. These lettuce seeds are available from R.H. Shumway, PO Box 1, Graniteville, SC 29829.

Sunflower, alfalfa, mung beans, lentil; all can be sprouted indoors or out. Soak, rinse, keep damp, wait. That's all.

Salad herbs can be grown in your garden or window box. Suggest: basil, chives, cilantro, dill, fennel, marjoram, mustard, parsley, rosemary, tarragon.

Not a salad herb but one that grows in abundance near us... bay leaves. Send a SASE to Bill Kaysing, PO Box 832, Soquel, CA 95073, and I'll return it with a handful of fresh bay. A fine addition for soups and stews.

Kim-Chi

Millions of Koreans would be willing to tell you that the best salad in the entire world is kim-chi. It's a hot, spicy sauerkraut, Oriental style. Make it yourself by chopping up several heads of Chinese cabbage into small pieces. Soak overnight in salted water. Drain but don't rinse. Mix in the following spices to your own taste: garlic, hot peppers, grated ginger. Pack into earthen jars, fill with water, add a heavy lid and store in a cool place for about 2 weeks. Then into the fridge while fermentation continues for another month or so. It's so tasty that you could become as addicted as the Koreans. Also, cost is laughable.

"Seeds are without doubt the greatest form of food for man or beast," to quote Robert Rodale, the organic gardening pioneer. And he's certainly right, for seeds contain all of the nutrients necessary to nourish the emerging plant embryo while its root system is developing. When you stop to think about it, some of our most nutritious staples, such as grains and legumes, are actually seeds.

But that's not all! There are several terrific seed bargains languishing around as snack food that we really ought to be taking more seriously. Most nuts, or seeds in a shell, are too expensive for a 99¢ a meal menu. But peanuts are a good buy, and sometimes walnuts too — and both are valuable sources of protein. Sesame and sunflower seeds make a wonderful nutrition booster in many dishes. Finally, there are many, many seeds that can be sprouted for a fresh, nutritious vegetable all year long.

NUTS & SEEDS

IT'S NOT JUST PEANUTS

Every once in a while we run across a sleeper in foods. For this book the sleeper is peanuts. Here we've been enjoying them for many years without realizing just how tremendously valuable they are in the human diet. In fact, peanuts are more than 20 percent pure protein! It's enlightening to see how much protein 100 grams of peanut butter (about 6 tablespoons) supplies compared to 100 grams of some other favorite protein foods: canned tuna gives you almost 29 grams of protein; peanut butter, almost 28; cooked hamburger, 24; creamed cottage cheese, about 13.5; scrambled eggs, about 11; and whole fluid milk, 3.5 (U.S. Department of Agriculture figures). As you can see, peanut butter rates well, even against heavy competition like this. It's also a good source of calcium, phosphorus, iron, and B-complex vitamins.

Do remember, though, that in order for your body to make the best use of all that peanut protein, you should be eating some beans and milk products along with it. In this way you'll be getting a better balance of all eight amino acids. For those who are overweight, peanuts should be used as a condiment or seasoning rather than a main food item, since they are high in calories. But if you're worried about cholesterol, you don't have to worry about peanuts. Oily as they are, they contain no cholesterol at all.

Peanuts are usually pretty pure, too. When I'm in a strange community with only a supermarket for a food source, I go in and get a bag of peanuts in the shell. That way I'm assured of getting food with minimum meddling plus maximum nutritional benefits. If you buy large quantities of peanuts to store, you must keep them in the refrigerator to prevent them from turning rancid. The same goes for peanut butter.

Once you get all those cheap peanuts home, what do you do with them? Here are some tips to get you started.

How to Handle a Peanut

Blanched Peanuts: Put shelled, raw peanuts into boiling water and let them stand 3 minutes. Drain. Slide the skins off with your fingers, and spread the nuts on absorbent paper to dry.

Peanut Alert

Moldy peanuts can contain aflatoxin which is a poison and carcinogen. So check your purchase carefully. Also, it might be wise to grind your own butter from perfect peanuts. When in doubt, throw them out.

French Fried Peanuts: You may fry the peanuts either in deep oil with a wire basket or in shallow oil with no basket. Put enough good vegetable oil into your pan to cover the peanuts. Heat the oil to 300° and add blanched peanuts. Stir them occasionally to ensure even cooking. As soon as the peanuts begin to brown, remove them from the oil, since they will continue to brown while cooling. Drain the peanuts and spread them on absorbent paper. Salt them to taste, using finely ground popcorn salt for the best results.

Roasted Shelled Peanuts: Put blanched peanuts in one layer deep in a shallow baking pan. Roast them at 350° for 15 to

20 minutes until they're golden brown, stirring occasionally. Flavor them with melted butter and salt to taste.

Roasted Peanuts in the Shell: Put peanuts one or two layers deep in a shallow baking pan. Roast them at 350° for 25 to 30 minutes, stirring occasionally. During the last few minutes of roasting time, shell and taste one to find out whether they're done.

Your Own Peanut Butter: Grind the desired quantity of fresh raw or roasted peanuts in your blender, adding a bit of vegetable oil as you blend to achieve the desired consistency. Salt to taste.

Baked Peanut Butter Chicken

1-3 pound chicken, cut in pieces
$^1/_4$ cup whole wheat flour
1 egg
$^1/_3$ cup peanut butter
1 teaspoon salt
$^1/_8$ teaspoon pepper
$^1/_3$ cup milk
$^1/_2$ cup bread crumbs
$^1/_4$ cup peanut oil

Wash and dry the chicken pieces. Dip them in flour. Blend the egg, peanut butter, salt, and pepper with a fork. Gradually add the milk. Dip the floured chicken pieces in this mixture and then in the bread crumbs. Place them on an oiled baking pan and drizzle the remaining oil over the chicken. Bake at 375° for 45 minutes. Serves 4.

Peanut Sweet Potatoes

4 medium sweet potatoes
$^2/_3$ cup milk
$^1/_4$ cup peanut butter
$^1/_2$ teaspoon salt
$^1/_2$ cup chopped roasted peanuts

Bake the potatoes for 45 minutes in a 350° oven, or until done. Cut them in half, scoop out the shells, and mash the potato with the milk, peanut butter, and salt. Refill the shells with the mixture, sprinkle the chopped peanuts on top, and return them to the oven until the sweet potato mixture is lightly browned. Serves 6-8.

Peanuts are easy to grow. Plant seeds 1 to 2 inches deep, 6 inches apart, after all danger of frost. Soil should be well-drained, sandy and loose. Thin seedlings to 8 to 12 inches apart. Before frost, dig up entire plant and air dry. Courtesy Shumway Seeds, PO Box 1, Graniteville, SC 29829.

It's Not Just for Sandwiches

There are endless ways to use peanut butter besides the traditional peanut butter sandwich.

- Mix it with ground meat to add a new flavor dimension and stretch your dollar farther.
- Add it to biscuit and cake batter.
- Try it in creamed soups for extra flavor and a nutritional boost.
- A dressing made of peanut butter thinned with milk is delicious on vegetables. Add a little honey and you'll find it's superb on fruit salad.
- Peanut butter pudding can be out of this world!

- If you do decide to make some sandwiches, skip the jelly and try some more nutritious companions for your peanut butter.
- Peanut butter can be combined with soft cheeses, grated carrot, or mashed banana for a delicious sandwich spread.
- It's a good base for smorgasbord sandwiches with lettuce or sprouts, tomato, anchovies, meats, or what-have-you.
- On whole-wheat toast, with cottage cheese, it makes a great quick high-protein breakfast.

Peanut Carrot Salad

2 cups coarsely grated carrots
lemon juice to taste (about 1 teaspoon)
1 cup chopped roasted peanuts
$^1/_2$ cup raisins.
mayonnaise
lettuce leaves
orange sections

Sprinkle the carrots with a little lemon juice; then combine them with the peanuts, raisins, and mayonnaise. Serve on lettuce leaves, garnished with orange sections. Serves 6.

Peanut Corn Cakes

1 cup cooked corn
$^1/_2$ cup milk
1 egg
1 cup corn meal
1 teaspoon baking powder
$^3/_4$ teaspoon salt
$^1/_3$ cup chopped roasted peanuts

Whirl the corn in a blender with the milk and egg. Add it to the dry ingredients along with the peanuts. Drop by table-spoonfuls onto a hot griddle and brown on both sides. Serve with molasses. Makes 6-8 cakes.

Peanut Rice

$^3/_4$ cup chopped roasted peanuts
1 cup sliced celery
$^1/_4$ cup chopped onion
3 tablespoons peanut oil
$^1/_2$ teaspoon thyme
salt and pepper
1 cup raw brown rice
3 cups water or broth

Sauté the peanuts and vegetables in oil in a heavy frying pan for 5 minutes. Add the thyme, salt and pepper, and rice, and cook for another 5 minutes, stirring occasionally. Add the water or broth, bring to a boil, turn down the heat, and simmer covered for 40 minutes or until the rice is tender. Serves 4.

Peanut Bread

2 cups raw ground peanuts
2 cups whole-wheat flour
$^1/_2$ teaspoon sea salt
2 teaspoons baking powder
2 eggs
$^2/_3$ cup milk
$^1/_2$ cup oil
$^1/_2$ cup honey
1 teaspoon vanilla

Mix the peanuts into the dry ingredients. Beat the eggs with the milk, oil, honey, and vanilla. Add the liquids to the dry ingredients, and stir just until well mixed. Bake in a greased and floured loaf pan for 45 minutes at 350°. Makes 1 loaf.

Cracker Jack

When I was small and living in South Pasadena, California, my cure for all ailments, physical, emotional and otherwise, was a nice fresh box of Cracker Jack. Not only did one enjoy the molasses-coated popcorn, there were a few roasted peanuts as a bonus feature. And to crown the nickel bargain, there was a surprise — a puzzle, toy figure or other small amusement.

I calculate that from 1925 until 1935, at least 30 percent of my bloodstream was pure essence of Cracker Jack. And I attribute my longevity to this miraculous cure-all.

Roast small peanuts with skins on. Boil a mixture of corn syrup, with molasses to taste, to stiff-ball stage. Pour over desired quantity of popped corn/peanuts and stir with a wooden spoon until well mixed. Allow to cool and then dive in! While enjoying this treat, think of all the money you're saving. NOTE: Go easy on the sweetening and you can serve this as a breakfast cereal.

WALNUTS: LOW-COST LUXURY

Walnuts have been well known and loved since ancient times. It's generally thought that they originated in Persia and spread from there to Carthage and Egypt. They were also cultivated in Constantinople, and remains of them have been found in Roman villas.

The Romans called walnuts "the royal nut" or "the nut of Jupiter." They used them not only for food but for medicinal purposes and dyeing. In Germany, so the story goes, young farmers used to prove their readiness for marriage by demonstrating that they had grown a certain number of walnut trees.

Of course, walnuts finally made their way from the Mediterranean area and Europe to America. And we're happy to say that of late, this venerable nut has been pretty cheap over here! Apparently the warehouses are full and the supply has exceeded the demand, driving the price down.

Should this situation continue, or whenever you do notice walnuts being offered at a low price, buy up several pounds. They will keep in the shell for quite a while — at least a year — and can be shelled just before using. (If you do shell any ahead of time, be sure to keep them in the refrigerator to prevent them from turning rancid.) Walnuts add such a marvelous flavor and crunch to so many dishes that we would hate to be without them. As with many of the other varieties of nuts, walnuts are a good protein provider. Here is a main dish you might like to try, along with a few other suggestions for using this ancient nut.

(If you live in a part of the country where some other variety of nut happens to be more plentiful or cheaper, feel free to substitute it for walnuts in any of our recipes.)

Walnut Dinner Loaf

1 small onion, minced
1 tablespoon butter
1 cup cooked beans
1 cup chopped walnuts
1 egg
1 teaspoon sage
salt and pepper to taste
1 cup toasted bread crumbs

Brown the onion in the butter until soft. Add the cooked beans, walnuts, egg, sage, salt and pepper, and bread crumbs. If the mixture seems too stiff, add a little more water. If it's too soft, add more bread crumbs. Turn it into a buttered baking pan and bake at 350° for 40 minutes. Serve with leftover gravy or a tomato sauce. Serves 6.

Vegetable-Nut Salad with Apples

Combine equal amounts of the following chopped ingredients: carrots, cucumber, green pepper, celery, apples, and walnuts. Toss together with sufficient mayonnaise to moisten.

Honey-Walnut Syrup

Here's one of our favorite toppings for pancakes or waffles. Stir together in a saucepan equal parts of honey and butter until the butter is melted. Add plenty of chopped walnuts and pour the syrup into a serving bowl with a large spoon for ladling over freshly baked waffles or pancakes.

This beats any overpriced, phony maple-flavored sugar syrup you can buy, and it will keep your energy up until way past lunchtime, especially if you serve it over our Pantry Pancakes (see page 10.)

California Walnut Bread

Here's the old-fashioned walnut bread, a classic among recipes.

3 cups whole-wheat flour
1 cup date sugar or $^1/_2$ cup honey
2 teaspoons baking powder
pinch of salt
$1^1/_2$ cups coarsely chopped walnuts
3 eggs, beaten
$^1/_2$ cup skim milk made from dry powder
$^1/_4$ cup oil
1 teaspoon vanilla

Toss the flour, date sugar, baking powder, and salt into the mixing bowl. Stir in the walnuts, then the eggs, milk, oil, and vanilla. Mix until just blended. Turn into a greased and floured 9x5x3-inch loaf pan. Sprinkle a few walnut halves over the top. Bake at 350° for about 1 hour. Let the loaf stand for 10 minutes. Then turn it onto a wire rack to cool.

For variations, add $^3/_4$ cup mashed bananas, a cup of chopped fresh raw cranberries, or a cup of coarsely chopped raisins, dates, prunes, or apricots. You may have to adjust the liquid a bit to compensate, but remember, stir gently.

The San Fernando Valley still had walnut orchards when we lived there in the 60s. So as soon as the harvesters had picked, we would go in and gather up the windfalls. Nothing tasted so good as a freshly-cracked, just-off-the-tree walnut. Always went back home with at least two full shopping bags.

Pumpkin-Walnut Cookies

Here's a good way to use some of that free pumpkin we hope you picked up after Halloween. Also, these cookies are especially nice to have on hand for the holiday season.

$^1/_2$ cup oil
$^3/_4$ cup honey
2 eggs
1 cup cooked pumpkin
1 teaspoon vanilla
1 teaspoon lemon juice
1 teaspoon grated lemon peel
$2^1/_2$ cups whole-wheat flour
2 teaspoons baking powder
pinch of salt
1 tablespoon pumpkin pie spice
$^1/_4$ teaspoon ginger
$^1/_2$ teaspoon cinnamon
1 cup coarsely chopped walnuts

Mix the oil and honey, and beat in the eggs one at a time. Stir in the pumpkin, vanilla, lemon juice and peel. Mix the flour with the baking powder, salt, and spices, and blend into the liquid ingredients. Stir in the walnuts and drop by teaspoonfuls onto a greased cookie sheet. Bake at 375° for 12 to 14 minutes. Makes about 6 dozen.

Walnuts Are Storable

And this thought evokes the fact that 99¢ a meal food is often just that... eminently storable.

We live in an era of fast changes. Who really knows when your regular food suppliers will be out... for a week, a month or longer. Obviously, it makes good sense to have something on hand. Here are some items we keep around:

Rice, both brown and white.
Wheat, whole grain. Some was found in Egyptian tombs still good.
Corn, also in whole-kernel form.
Honey, a source of quick energy that keeps forever.
Dates, another nutritious and long-lasting item.
Raisins and Prunes, ideal for storage and useful in menus.

We put the grains in clean gallon bottles dropping in a lighted piece of paper to evacuate the remaining oxygen. Seal quickly.

Honey and dried fruits go into metal containers tightly sealed and all stored in a cool dry place.

Sesame,
Sunflower & Co.

Among the many edible seeds, there are two we use most often — sesame and sunflower. These can be valuable sources of protein, particularly when you combine them with beans or dairy products.

Available in any well-stocked natural food store, sesame seeds are useful and tasty. Sprinkle a thin layer on a cookie sheet and toast them at low heat in the oven. They are then delicious eaten just plain or sprinkled on hot cereals, on rolls before baking, on soups or stews, or practically anyplace where you need more flavor and nutritional value.

You can make your own tahini sauce, too (see our recipe on page 119). Tahini's not only perfect for your falafels; it can be used as a spread for sandwiches, as a flavoring for dishes such as stews and soups, as a dressing for soyburgers, or anyplace where you want some really fine flavor to spark up an otherwise bland dish. Another easy way to use sesame seeds is simply to toss a handful into your blender when you are making smoothies or health drinks. They will add just that little touch of crunchiness that tastes so good in a malt-like drink, plus extra protein.

Our other favorite eating seed, the sunflower seed, is an important crop for the Russians, who plant millions of acres every year. Their acreage, as well as ours, is increasing as more and more people become acquainted with this valuable food. Sunflower seeds can be purchased hulled or unhulled. In the hulled state, they're ready to add to any dish or simply to eat out of your hand. Keep them and any other shelled seeds in the refrigerator. In the unhulled state, you have a good time-passer while you're waiting for the Second Coming!

An interesting fact about sunflowers is that they face toward the sun all day long and then turn back to dawn position during the night. (I haven't stayed up all night to watch them do it, but I know it's true because if they didn't, they would wring their own green necks.)

We'd like just to mention some other seeds you might want to experiment with:

- pumpkin or squash (toast them — they're great snack food)
- poppy, caraway, anise, celery, dill (all for seasoning)
- fenugreek (makes a wonderful tea, better still with a few drops of honey)

Now for some favorite recipes using our favorite seeds.

Sunflower-Oat Waffles

1 cup rolled oats
2 cups hot water
1 cup whole-wheat flour
$^1/_2$ cup milk powder
1 egg, beaten
2 tablespoons oil
2 tablespoons honey
2 teaspoons baking powder
$^1/_2$ teaspoon sea salt
$^2/_3$ cup sunflower seeds

Pour the hot water over the oats and let them stand until softened. Add the remaining ingredients, blending well, and bake in a hot waffle iron.

These can be topped with homemade applesauce sweetened with honey and flavored with cinnamon. Molasses and honey are also good toppings. Makes about 6 waffles.

Sesame Seed Pilaf

$^1/_4$ cup sesame seeds
4 tablespoons butter or margarine
1 large onion, chopped
1 clove garlic, minced
1 cup raw brown rice
2 cups chicken stock
1 cup fresh shelled peas, or 1 package frozen peas

Toast the sesame seeds over low heat in a medium-sized saucepan, stirring frequently until they turn golden. Pour them out of the pan and set them aside.

In the pan melt the butter or margarine and add the onion and garlic. Cook over low heat, stirring, until the onion is soft and yellow. Add the rice and cook a few minutes longer, stirring constantly. Add the stock, bring to a boil, stir once, then cover and simmer for 20 to 25 minutes or until the rice is tender. Add the peas and the toasted sesame seeds, and cook gently until the peas are done, stirring occasionally. Salt to taste. Serves 3-4.

Sesame Cauliflower

1 head cauliflower
$^1/_4$ cup sesame seeds
4 tablespoons butter
1 small onion, minced
$^1/_4$ cup water
$^1/_2$ cup sliced green onions
$^1/_4$ cup chopped parsley
salt and pepper
lemon wedges

Cut out the hard central core from the cauliflower, separate the flowerettes, and slice them. Brown the sesame seeds in 2 tablespoons of butter, stirring frequently. Set aside.

Sauté the cauliflower and onion in the remaining butter until almost tender; add the water, cover, and steam a few more minutes until done. Stir in the green onions, parsley, and sesame seeds. Squeeze lemon over the cauliflower when serving. Serves 6.

Lemon-Poppy Seed Bread

1 tablespoon poppy seeds
$^1/_2$ cup milk
2 cups whole-wheat pastry flour
1 tablespoon baking powder
1 teaspoon salt
1 cup oil
$^1/_2$ cup honey
2 eggs
1 tablespoon grated lemon rind

Combine the poppy seeds and milk, and set them aside. Mix the dry ingredients. Combine the oil and honey, and gradually beat in the eggs. Add the dry ingredients alternately with the milk to the oil-honey-egg mixture. Stir in the lemon rind. Pour the batter into a greased loaf pan and bake at 350° for 45 minutes or until done. Remove from the pan and cool on a wire rack. Makes 1 loaf.

Arabian Stuffed Cabbage

This recipe also calls for caraway seeds, which give it a wonderful exotic taste.

1 cup brown rice
1 large onion, chopped
2 tablespoons oil
$^1/_2$ cup toasted sunflower seeds
1 tablespoon caraway seeds
$^1/_4$ cup raisins
$^1/_2$ teaspoon salt
1 head cabbage
2 cups tomato sauce
1 cup yogurt

Cook the rice until tender. Sauté the onion in the oil and combine it with the rice; add the seeds, raisins, and salt. Core the cabbage and steam it for a few minutes until its leaves can be easily removed. Separate the leaves and place about 3 tablespoons of rice mixture in each. Roll the leaves up and skewer them with a toothpick if desired. Place them in a heavy iron skillet, pour the tomato sauce over them, and simmer for about 20 minutes. Serve topped with a dollop of yogurt. Serves 6-8.

Sunflower Seed Bread

1 package active dry yeast
2 tablespoons honey
$1^1/_2$ teaspoons salt
$3^1/_2$-4 cups whole wheat flour
$^1/_2$ cup milk
2 tablespoons butter
1 egg, beaten
1 tablespoon grated orange peel
$^1/_2$ cup orange juice
$^2/_3$ cup shelled sunflower seeds

In a bowl combine the yeast, honey, salt and $1^1/2$ cups flour. Heat the milk and butter to 115° (or lukewarm) and add them to the dry mixture. Add the egg, orange peel, and juice. Beat for several minutes, or until thoroughly blended.

Stir in the sunflower seeds by hand, and add enough flour to make a soft dough. Knead the dough for 5 or 6 minutes; then place it in a greased bowl, cover it with a light towel or cloth napkin, and let it rise in a warm place until doubled. Punch it down and let it rest 5 minutes.

Shape it into a loaf and place it in a greased 8½x4½-inch loaf pan. Cover and let rise again until double. Bake at 375° for 40 minutes. Remove the loaf from the pan immediately and brush the top with butter. Makes 1 loaf.

Sunflowers For Longevity

Did you know that parrots can live on just sunflower seeds and water — nothing else — for 100 years or more. Proof that this little seed has everything needed for this complex and talkative bird. And just think of the colors that those seeds must produce — a miracle of Mother Nature!

Sprouts For All Seasons

In the predecessor to this book, *Eat Well for 99¢ a Meal*, we discussed the fantastic food value and low cost of sprouts. They can be grown anywhere, anytime, without soil or sunshine. That means you can have fresh vegetables all year long. And they're just chock full of vitamins and minerals.

The list of sproutable seeds is long indeed. The tiny alfalfa seed is ideal for beginners, since it's so easy to sprout, and the sprouts taste so delightfully crunchy and delicate! We put a thick layer of them in our sandwiches in place of lettuce because they're so much more nutritious. They're also marvelous for salads and can be added at the last minute to hot dishes such as soups and vegetable casseroles.

The chia seed, also very tiny, was well known by the Indians, who often used it as trail food. When they were on long hunting trips, they would take along a pouchful of chia seeds and toss a small amount in their mouth from time to time. They held the seeds in their mouth without swallowing them to soften them and extract the nutrients. Though not used widely in any cooked form that we are aware of, chia seeds will produce delicate green sprouts which can be clipped and added to salads. If kept moist, the seeds will continue to sprout for a long time.

Ever wonder how Chinese restaurants can stay in business so persistently, rain or shine, depression or boom? It's because they serve lots of mung bean sprouts! A pound of mung beans costs about $2 as of this writing. When sprouted, they weigh more than 4 pounds. At this rate, a pound of sprouts costs something like 50 cents. So a generous plate of sprouts with a few slices of pork or beef and some sauce makes an economical dish that can sell for as low as $4 and still make a nice profit. The point is, the same economics can work for you at home, anytime you want to get started.

Here are some of the other seeds you might want to try sprouting for salads, bread sandwiches, or casseroles: beans (garbanzo, soy, kidney, navy, and so on), lentils, peas, sesame seeds, sunflower seeds, adzuki seeds, and even grains — wheat (see page 5), buckwheat, oats, barley, and rye.

Good News!

An indication that conventional food sources are getting more natural is displayed by the use of sprouts in sandwiches, salads, and other dishes. One can even find them in the salad buffets which have been proliferating at an accelerated pace. So it's SPROUTS TO THE RESCUE OF AMERICAN HEALTH!

Favorite Sprout Sandwich

Spread some homemade mayonnaise on two slices of whole-wheat bread. For the filling use a slice of cheese, a slice of avocado, a slice of tomato, and a thick layer of alfalfa sprouts. Cream cheese is especially good in this sandwich. Sprinkle a few sunflower seeds over the cheese, and you have a meal that will sustain you for hours.

How to Sprout Any Seed

1. Be sure the seeds are not coated with anything. Many seeds intended for planting have fungicide on them, and this would be harmful to eat.
2. Wash them anyway.
3. Pour a small quantity in a large jar, leaving plenty of room for expansion, and soak them overnight.
4. Drain them thoroughly and rinse them at least twice a day; three times is better. Keep them moist but not soggy. If they are too wet, they will rot.
5. To make it easy to rinse the seeds, put a piece of porous cloth — any old but clean nylon stocking works fine — over the top of the jar and hold it in place with a rubber band.
6. Store the sprouting seeds in a dark, fairly warm place. After all, you are simulating the environment of a seed sprouting in damp soil on a warm spring day.
7. In a few days, or less for small seeds, you will be pleased to observe developing roots and tops. You can eat the sprouts at any stage, raw or cooked, but they're more nutritious raw.
8. If you wish, you may increase the chlorophyll content of your sprouts by placing them in indirect sunlight for a few hours. Then store them in the refrigerator just like any other fresh vegetable.

Once you start this routine, you'll want to have a batch of sprouts going all the time. If you start some every couple of days, you will never be without a crunchy, nutritious supply.

99¢ a Meal Chop Suey

First make up 6 cups of mung-bean sprouts yourself. They will only cost about 80 cents. Then cook in a wok or frying pan:

2 large onions, chopped rather coarsely
1 medium stalk of celery, tops and all, sliced
a few mushrooms, sliced
6 cloves of garlic, minced

You can steam them with a bit of water in the bottom or add a teaspoon of sesame oil to prevent sticking and add flavor. Cook until tender. Now add the 6 cups of drained sprouts and cook only until they're warm and delicately tender. Serve with chopsticks and plenty of soy sauce — the authentic kind bought from a Chinese grocery. Serves 4, at a cost per serving of about 27 cents for a most generous dish.

Incidentally, this is a great party dish. People love it, and it's inexpensive and quite simple to make. If you want to dress it up, add a few slivers of cooked pork or beef just before serving.

If you have extra guests arriving unexpectedly, add two or three cups of warmed Chinese noodles.

Sprout Omelet

3 eggs, beaten
2 green onions with tops, sliced
2 tablespoons oil or butter
$^3/_4$ cup sprouts (mung-bean, lentil, adzuki, alfalfa)
salt and pepper to taste

Sauté the sliced green onions in the oil until almost tender, add the sprouts, and pour the beaten eggs over the top. Cook the omelet gently until set; then fold it over and finish cooking or place it under a broiler flame to brown the uncooked portion. Serve it in wedges. A mixture of sprouts may be used. Serves 2 liberally.

Sprout-Mushroom Quiche

1 cup sliced mushrooms
$^1/_2$ onion, sliced
$^1/_4$ cup oil
$^3/_4$ cup favorite sprouts
9-inch whole-wheat pie shell
2 eggs, beaten
1 cup milk
$^1/_2$ cup grated cheese
1 teaspoon sea salt

Sauté the mushrooms and onion in the oil. Add the sprouts, and spread the vegetables into the pie shell. Blend the eggs, milk, cheese, and salt, and pour them over the vegetables. Bake at 350° for 25 to 30 minutes. Serves 4-6.

Chinese Vegetable Medley

Another Chinese dish using sprouts, but this time not quite so many.

$^1/_2$ cup vegetable oil
1 cup diagonally sliced celery
$^1/_2$ cup sliced broccoli or cauliflower
$^1/_2$ cup sliced mushrooms
1 large onion, sliced
$^1/_2$ bunch spinach or chard leaves
1 cup mung bean sprouts
soy sauce to taste

Wash and slice all the vegetables, and arrange them conveniently near your stove before you begin cooking. Heat the oil over a high flame in a wok or large heavy frying pan. Add the celery and broccoli or cauliflower, and stir fry (fry while stirring briskly with a spatula or wooden spoon) for a few minutes; then add the mushrooms and onion, continuing to stir fry until almost tender. Add the spinach or chard leaves and sprouts last, and stir fry a few more minutes. The vegetables should be barely tender. Add soy sauce to taste and serve over noodles or brown rice. Serves 4.

This recipe can be varied according to what vegetables you have on hand. For example, asparagus, carrots, string beans, or any kind of summer squash could be substituted for any of the vegetables above. But of course, you'll always have your sprouts!

Spark Up Your Foods With Seasonings

There is hardly a city or town in the world that doesn't have at least one Chinese restaurant. Why are chop suey and its tablemates so popular? After all, most of what you are eating is sprouts and noodles. The secret is seasoning... all those great Chinese flavorings like ginger, hot peppers and sesame oil interwoven with skills derived from 40 centuries of culinary experimentation.

Here are some of the basic seasonings from all over the globe. Enjoy your own experiments.

Sesame Oil: This is absolutely wonderful stuff. Although it is expensive, so little is required to enhance any veggie dish, it's actually a bargain.

Shoyu: One of the many soy sauces that give the illusion of meat. Go easy as there is often a lot of salt in soy.

Miso: Essentially a solid form of fermented soy beans often used as a basis for soups and sauces. In many varieties.

Jalapeño: One of the many hot peppers to pep up the bland basics like corn and beans. Just one chopped jalapeño can enhance a whole pan of refried beans.

Horseradish: A positively marvelous perker-upper. Considered an adjunct to meat it can be used for many dishes needing some culinary aid.

Béarnaise Sauce: Just one of the many unique French innovations composed of mayonnaise, mustard, tarragon vinegar, and shallots, all whirled in a blender. (What did we ever do without them?)

Aioli: A mixture of a large crushed garlic clove, 2 egg yolks mixed well and followed by $^1/_2$ cup olive oil added slowly until mixture thickens. Tremendous when spread on hot baguettes.

Sauce for Sourdough Chunks: Pour some virgin olive oil into a small saucer. Add a couple of splashes of balsamic vinegar and mix. Dip your bread and enjoy. Sounds expensive but if you buy the two ingredients wholesale, it won't break your budget.

During the summer of 1976, Bill and several friends lived on the venerable Coast Guard cutter-turned-houseboat, The Flying Goose. While on board they rediscovered some ancient Aztec, Toltec, and Inca truths, including:

- Corn is a great provider of strength and flavor (and it's cheap too, especially when purchased in 100-pound sacks).
- Corn and beans, when combined with such goodies as tomatoes, chilies, and crisp greens, can create a superb diet that never bores the tastebuds.

Best of all is a little bit of modern wisdom: the combination of corn and beans makes a complete protein!

Although our summer cuisine emphasized Mexican food, you don't really have to cook Mexican style to discover corn and beans. Many of the

CORN & BEANS

corn recipes that follow are actually traditional dishes in the United States. Likewise, the bean recipes in the second section could be identified with numerous areas of the globe. Continuing on the bean theme, we've rounded out this section with two more chapters containing recipes for our beloved garbanzos and the incomparable soybean.

Amazing Maize

If you want some free corn along toward late summer, find a cornfield that's just been harvested and ask the owner if you can glean the missed ears. They're easy to shuck and shell, and if you have children it can be fun for them to see just where corn really comes from and how it can be prepared to eat without the intercession of the food industry.

You may not have a nearby cornfield to glean from. In that case your solution is a nice big sack of dried whole-kernel corn, which only costs about $15 for 50 pounds these days. Once you begin working with it, you'll find more and more uses for this versatile, totally delicious food.

For fresh corn meal, simply grind some in your trusty blender. Remember that corn meal can be substituted with excellent results for part of the ordinary flour in many recipes, such as those for waffles and pancakes. The recipes that follow will set you on the path to enjoying more of this important food.

Parched Corn

The American Indians of long ago often depended on parched corn for sustenance. Handy when you're on the trail, parched corn is easy to make, delicious to eat, and low, low in cost.

White corn is the best to use, though just about any variety of dried corn will do. Spread a layer on a cookie sheet and put it in your oven the next time you bake potatoes or beans. The corn will roast or "parch" and become digestible. Salt it if you like.

An alternative method is similar to popping popcorn. Just add the corn to an oiled pan and dry or toast it gently, being careful not to burn it. Parched corn stores virtually forever; it's good ground up as a cereal; and it may be used just as you would use any kernel corn, if you wish.

Corn for Health

A few months after the first edition of this book was published, I ran into an old friend.

He was full of enthusiasm as he told me this story. After reading the chapter on corn he decided to eat almost nothing but corn for a given period of time.

First of all, he was delighted with the all-corn menu and was never bored.

Second, he noticed a great improvement in his overall health. He had more energy, could think more clearly and, in general, felt like a new person.

My theory of what happened was that the corn acted like a giant internal broom, sweeping all the toxins out of his system. Could happen to anyone, couldn't it?

Popcorn Reprise

Take advantage of this inexpensive food often. Buy it in bulk, pop it in an iron skillet with a little olive or soy oil, and add anything you like to the result. Salt and butter are standard, but it's fun to experiment with such deluxe touches as chopped almonds and honey, cashews and maple syrup, hazel nuts and date sugar, or peanuts and molasses.

Ground up in your blender or food mill, popcorn becomes a fabulous cereal which can be cooked and served with milk, dried fruits, or whatever you fancy. Once you try your own popcorn treats, you won't be tempted to pay two dollars or more for a package of ready-made ones in the supermarket. In fact, you'll pass them up with a righteous sneer.

Since we've gotten started on describing how you can make your own snack foods, here a few more.

Corn Crackers

These are much better for you than any store-bought crackers, and certainly much cheaper.

$1^1/2$ cups freshly ground corn meal
1 cup whole-wheat flour
$^1/2$ cup wheat germ
$^1/2$ teaspoon sea salt
1 teaspoon honey
$^1/2$ cup water
$^1/3$ cup oil

Mix the dry ingredients. Beat the honey, water, and oil together, and add them slowly to the dry mixture. Mix and knead lightly. Roll out the dough with a rolling pin as thinly as possible. If desired, sprinkle it with salt. Cut the dough into whatever size and shape you want, and place the crackers on a well-greased cookie sheet.

Bake them for 1 minute at 400°; then reduce the heat to 300° and bake for 25 minutes more. Remove them from the cookie sheet to cool, and try to keep from eating all of them at once.

Homemade Corn Chips

Put fresh corn tortillas in a 300° oven and bake them until they're crisp. Cook, break into bite-sized pieces, and store in an airtight jar. For a fraction of what you would pay for the oil-fried kind, you have a convenient chip for dips. (Thanks to our good friend Dan Clark for this dandy method.)

Indian Pudding Simplified

Mix $^1/_2$ pint water with $^1/_2$ pint milk and let boil in double boiler. Add $^2/_3$ cup fresh ground cornmeal, $^1/_2$ teaspoon salt and $^2/_3$ cup blackstrap molasses. Stir.

Boil until thick like porridge. Put into baking dish with 1 quart milk but do not stir. Bake at least two hours. Serve warm with yogurt topping. Mmmm!

Corn Crunchies

When you master this recipe, you'll be free of those over-priced, sugar-coated supermarket cereals forever.

1 cup water
1 cup corn meal, freshly ground from parched corn
$^1/_4$ cup safflower oil
1 cup brown rice, ground into flour
$^1/_2$ cup soy flour
$^1/_2$ cup wheat germ

Heat the water to a rolling boil and add the corn meal all at once. Remove from the fire and stir until mixed. Now add the safflower oil, rice and soy flour, and wheat germ. Knead lightly. The dough will be slightly crumbly. Spread it out on a lightly greased cookie sheet and bake until lightly browned in a moderate oven, stirring occasionally. Eat as is or add honey or other natural sweeteners. Serves 6.

Hot Cornbread with Wild Blackberries

Get up early to beat the competition to the blackberry bushes. Pick a quart or so. While you are gone have someone mix up this batter and stick it in the oven:

2 cups whole-wheat flour
2 cups freshly ground corn meal
pinch of sea salt
2 tablespoons baking powder
$^1/_2$ cup safflower or soy oil
$^1/_2$ cup honey, wild or domestic
skim milk

Sift the dry ingredients together. Blend the oil and honey, and add them to the dry ingredients. Add enough skim milk to make a fairly thick batter. Pour it into an oiled pan and bake it in a hot oven (about 400°) for about 25 minutes, or until a toothpick comes out clean.

Cool it slightly, slice it thickly, and spoon your crushed berries over the top. Sit down with the enormous appetite you've just worked up and enjoy! Serves 6.

Spoonbread

One of the more delectable variations on the cornbread theme. We've served it for breakfast, lunch, or dinner, and needed very little else to satisfy our inner persons.

$^1/_2$ cup corn meal
$^3/_4$ teaspoon sea salt
2 cups milk
2 eggs, separated
1 tablespoon oil
$1\,^1/_2$ teaspoons baking powder

Cook the corn meal and salt in the milk until thick. Remove from the heat. Beat the egg yolks and add them to the corn meal mixture along with the oil and baking powder. Beat the egg whites until stiff and fold them in. Pour the batter into a buttered casserole and bake it at 375° for 30 minutes. Serve warm. Serves 4.

Terrific Tortillas

Tortillas were the mainstay of our diet aboard the great "Flying Goose" during the experimental summer of '76. We bought them from a tortilleria in Brentwood, California, for the amazing low price of just 20 cents a dozen. These were fresh, limp, often warm from the oven! (What a treat compared to the conventional kind that lie in the supermarket caskets stiff and cold.)

Now there are many conventional things to do with tortillas. You can make them into enchiladas, tacos, tostados, and such. But have you ever thought of having them for breakfast? As I write these very words, I am sautéing a tortilla in a bit of butter (it could be soy oil or something else), and when it's hot and delicious, I'll spread a thick layer of some fine apple butter that a friend just gave me on the tortilla, roll it up, and eat it with gusto! I could just as well dribble a bit of honey on it (or maple syrup) and eat it like an American pancake. Or it could be the platter of a fried egg. But I'm sure you get the plan — just heat up a tortilla or two tomorrow morning and then let your imagination run riot. You'll be eating good food for pennies!

Hoecakes

The pioneers got their energy to build log cabins and plow rocky fields from 19th century staples like this. If you're looking for more vitality, try these tomorrow morning with lots of butter, chopped walnuts, and honey.

1¹/2 cups water
1¹/2 cups freshly ground corn meal
pinch of salt
1 teaspoon honey
¹/4 cup safflower oil
2 eggs

Boil the water in a heavy pot — the kind pioneers used for just about everything. Then add the corn meal, salt, and honey. Stir until the mixture becomes thick. Add the oil and eggs. Beat with great vigor (this will give you an appetite). Drop by tablespoonfuls onto a greased cookie sheet.

Bake for about ¹/2 hour at 375° or until nicely browned. Then serve them hot from the oven to the plaudits of the assembled. Makes 2 dozen.

If any hoecakes survive the first round (unlikely), they make a fine corn bun for almost any filling from peanut butter to melted cheese.

Handy Corn

If you keep a container of freshly-ground corn meal in your refrigerator you'll find lots of uses for it. Use it to bread fish or chicken parts. Also, toss into smoothies to add bulk and nutrition. It's perfect as a quick thickener of soups and stews. Add some to every pancake or muffin recipe. Enjoy!

Polenta San Joaquin

1 quart water
1 cup yellow corn meal
1 teaspoon salt

Bring the water to boil and slowly add the corn meal and salt, beating with a wire whisk to avoid lumps. Cook 5 minutes over medium heat; then turn the heat low and cook another 15 minutes, stirring frequently. Turn out onto a platter and serve with Italian Tomato Sauce (see page 13). Serves 4.

May be chilled and sliced. Sauté in butter.

Hot Corn Meal Mush

Grind some dried corn in your blender. Soak it overnight. The next morning get up early and simmer it gently for about 1 hour. Serve it piping hot with honey, wild or domestic. Milk can be poured on for those who need it, but we learned to enjoy our mush au naturel.

Or, if you want to sleep in, you can prepare your mush the night before, and put it in the refrigerator. The next morning just slice it and fry the slices in safflower or another good vegetable oil. Serve with scrambled eggs to which a bit of fresh basil has been added.

Bradford Island Corn Cakes

Grind some dried corn in a blender or mill. Mix it with water to make a thin paste and pour it out on a hot, greased griddle. Flip the cakes as soon as set, and cook them on the other side until crisp. Serve immediately with crushed berries, sliced apples, or other fresh or cooked fruit.

Your Own Tortillas

While they are cheap to buy, you can make your own for less. Boil whole corn with a little lime and remove as much of the skin as possible. Grind with blender or mortar and pestle to a fine dough. Put a walnut-sized ball of dough between two pieces of parchment paper or plastic and flatten. You can also use a tortilla maker available from Mexican stores. Toast on hot skillet until done. Can be used immediately or stored in the refrigerator or frozen. We highly recommend this method, as many tortillas now have preservatives.

An alternative is to buy masa dough from a Mexican grocery. Save the first-step labor.

Pop Some Daily

Can't think of a better food than freshly-popped popcorn, preferably organic. We pop it for breakfast and often toss it in the blender for an easy-to-eat treat.

We bought some shakers with large openings and filled them with various mixes:

Parmesan, basil and cayenne, which creates Poppacorna.
Chili powder, cumin and cayenne, for Mexipop.
Dill, for Picklepop.
Ground caraway and Jarlsberg cheese, for Der Guten Poppen.
Cinnamon, ginger, nutmeg and date sugar, for Fantasycorn.

You can take it from here. Incidentally, we either dry pop or use olive oil in a heavy iron skillet. And olive oil is our choice over melted butter.

And we're serious about eating popcorn daily. Once you start, it will become a healthy, 99¢ a meal habit.

Beans, Beans, Beans

Beans store extremely well, so buy what you think you'll need for a year or two from a wholesale house. We once found one in Stockton, California, which sold us 100-pound sacks of beans for less than $25 each. In fact, we bought some slightly off-beat pintos for 14 cents a pound. You can afford to be generous with your chili when you buy them for that price!

Here are some of our recipes featuring beans as a mainstay. Some are Mexican, reflecting Bill's Mexican-inspired culinary summer aboard ship, but many are not. Note that in addition to that splendid combination of corn and beans, we have several dishes based on a close runner-up, rice and beans, which is another excellent protein combination.

Blowtorch Chili Beans

2 cups dried pinto or kidney beans
1 teaspoon sea salt
$^1/_4$ cup soy sauce
chili powder as you like it
$^1/_2$ teaspoon cumin
$^1/_2$ cup fresh tomato puree

Cover the beans with plenty of water and cook them over medium heat for about 2 hours or until tender. During the last half hour of cooking, stir in the remaining ingredients. Serves 4-6.

Bravo Bean Salad

This delicious summer concoction costs so little per serving that you won't believe it.

4 cups cooked red kidney beans, drained
1 cup sharp French dressing
1 cup celery, sliced
$^1/_2$ cup onion, chopped
garlic salt and freshly ground pepper to taste
onion rings and radish slices for garnish

Toss the first four ingredients gently, cover, and refrigerate. At serving time, drain off any excess dressing. Heap the mixture in a serving bowl and sprinkle it with garlic salt and freshly ground pepper. Taste, and add a little wine vinegar if needed. Garnish with onion rings and radish slices. Serves 4.

Black Bean-Rice Casserole

$^1/_2$ cup dried black beans
$^2/_3$ cup raw brown rice
1 teaspoon sea salt
$^1/_2$ teaspoon dry mustard
1 tablespoon molasses
1 tablespoon honey
$^3/_4$ cup yogurt
$^3/_4$ cup wheat germ

Cook the beans and rice separately in water to cover. Drain. Mix them together and add all the remaining ingredients except $1/4$ cup of the wheat germ. Place the mixture in a greased casserole, sprinkle the remaining wheat germ on top, and bake at 350° for 20 to 25 minutes. Serves 4-6.

It's difficult to think of a more valuable assist to the 99¢ a meal concept than the full spectrum of beans. Cheap to buy, easy to prepare and loaded with nutrition. Limas are the most valuable of all beans and in terms of weight and volume, give the most food value.

Lima Bean Casserole

2 cups dried lima beans
1 onion, chopped
2 cloves garlic, minced
$1/4$ cup oil
1 cup fresh tomatoes, chopped
1 teaspoon sea salt
1 teaspoon dill weed
paprika
$2/3$ cup grated cheddar cheese

Cook the lima beans in water to cover for about 2 hours or until tender, adding extra water as needed. Drain. Sauté the onion and garlic briefly in the oil and add them along with the tomatoes and seasonings to the lima beans in a greased casserole. Sprinkle the grated cheese on top and stir it in partially. Bake at 375° for 25 minutes. Serves 6.

Flying Goose Carte du Jour

Breakfast
  Hot Corn Meal Mush* with wild honey,
  or, Bradford Island Corn Cakes,*
  or, Hot Corn Meal Mush* with scrambled eggs,
  or, Hot Cornbread with Wild Blackberries*

Lunch
  Polenta San Joaquin,*
  or, Vegetable soup with leftover corn cakes,
  or, Delta scrapple (never the same twice),
  or, Super Bean Taco*

Dinner
  Enterprise tostadas,
  or, Blowtorch Chili Beans,*
  or, Enchilada Beans*

(With entrees like these, you can see that even allowing for the necessary extras — mainly beverages and lots of fruit — we were eating well for 99¢ a meal.)
* Recipe given.

Black-Eyed Peas and Rice

1 cup dried black-eyed peas
2 medium onions, chopped
$^1/_2$ green pepper, diced
1 clove garlic, minced
salt and pepper
1 cup raw brown rice
pinch of thyme
1 bay leaf, crumbled

Wash the dried peas and soak them overnight in cold water, or boil them for 2 minutes and soak them for 1 hour. Drain them, cover with boiling water, and add the onions, green pepper, garlic, and salt and pepper. Cook until the beans are soft (about 1 hour).

Add the rice, thyme, and bay leaf, and 2 more cups of boiling water. Cover and simmer for about 25 minutes or until the rice is done. Serves 6.

Enchilada Beans

2 tortillas
2 tablespoons vegetable oil
$^1/_3$ cup grated cheese
$1^1/_2$ cups cooked black-eyed peas
salt and pepper

Make cheese enchiladas by frying the tortillas in the oil until softened, filling them with some of the cheese, and rolling them up. Season the black-eyed peas with the salt and pepper, spread them in a shallow greased baking dish, and place the two cheese enchiladas on top. Sprinkle more grated cheese on top, cover the dish with foil, and bake at 375° for about 25 minutes. Then uncover and bake about 10 minutes longer. Serves 2.

Lentil-Nut Loaf

2 onions, chopped
2 stalks celery, chopped
3 cloves garlic, minced
2 cups bread crumbs
$^1/_4$ cup oil
3 cups cooked lentils
$^1/_4$ cup parsley, chopped

2 teaspoons thyme
2 teaspoons sage
$^1/_4$ cup soy sauce
1 teaspoon sea salt
1 tablespoon brewer's yeast
1 cup chopped nuts

Sauté the onions, celery, garlic, and $1^1/_2$ cups of bread crumbs in the oil for a few minutes. Mix the rest of the ingredients together, combine them with the sautéed mixture, and press into a greased loaf pan or baking dish. Spread the remaining $^1/_2$ cup of crumbs over the top, cover, and bake at 350° for $^1/_2$ hour.

Uncover and continue baking until the crumbs are browned. This can be served with tomato sauce, mushroom sauce, white sauce, or béchamel sauce. Serves 6.

Super Bean Tacos

Everyone is familiar with the basic American-version taco, filled with spiced meat, lettuce, tomatoes, and a sprinkling of grated cheese. But how about forgetting that expensive meat and substituting a generous portion of hot refried beans? They'll be cheaper, and they'll still make a complete protein when combined with the corn in your tortilla.

To make them, boil the desired quantity of beans (usually pinto) until tender in lightly salted water. Mash with cumin to taste, adding a tablespoon of melted lard for each cup of beans. Cool and let the flavors blend. Now reheat them and they're ready to use.

By adding the usual lettuce, tomato, and cheese to a bean taco, you'll have a delicious blend of flavors and textures at a lower cost. I estimate the cost of a meat taco to be about three times the cost of a bean taco.

Bean Loaf with Tomato-Cheese Sauce

1 onion, chopped
2 tablespoons vegetable oil
1^1/2 cups cooked beans, chopped
1 cup raw carrot, grated
2 eggs, beaten
1 teaspoon sea salt, sage
^{1}/2 teaspoon oregano
3 tablespoons brewer's yeast

Sauté the onion in the oil until tender. Combine it with all the remaining ingredients and put the mixture in an oiled loaf pan. Bake at 350° for 1 hour. Make the sauce as follows:

2 tablespoons butter
2 tablespoons whole-wheat flour
2 cups milk
3 ounces tomato paste
1 teaspoon salt
^{1}/3 cup grated Parmesan cheese

Blend the first three ingredients, and add the last three. Then heat the sauce in a pan, stirring constantly until smooth. Pour half of it over the bean loaf during the last 10 minutes of baking. Reserve the other half to pour over individual servings. Serves 4.

Boston Baked Beans
(In a crock pot)

3 cups small pea beans
^{1}/2 pound bacon
4 teaspoons honey
^{1}/3 cup molasses
Mustard, salt, pepper to taste
1 onion

Soak beans overnight. Rinse and cover with fresh water. Mix other ingredients with hot water and add to beans. Bury onion in center. Add water to top off crock, cover and bake in slow oven (250° F) for 8 hours.

Mexican Groceries

We live along the central coast of California where there are many Mexican residents and also many Mexican grocery stores. This is a great boon for us as we are fond of both the people and their food.

The stores all feature large bags of corn, masa farina (tortilla mix), beans of all kinds and plenty of dry chilis. There are also Mexican specialties like their famous chocolate mixed with cinnamon.

There are also cookware items like tortilla presses and mortar and pestles.

We hope you find one or a similar store in your area... it can greatly enhance your 99¢ a meal capability.

Garbanzo or Chick Peas

Anyone who likes Italian minestrone soup is already acquainted with garbanzos or chick peas. They are the round carmel-colored beans found in the bottom of every bowl. Garbanzos are also extremely popular in the Middle East, where they're used in the tasty falafels now finding their way into American craft fairs as well as small ethnic and vegetarian restaurants. For those who would like to make their own, here's how.

Falafels

2 cups dried garbanzo beans
$^{1}/_{2}$ cup water
1 clove garlic
2 tablespoons parsley
$^{1}/_{4}$ teaspoon cumin
1 teaspoon salt
1 cup bread crumbs

Wash the garbanzos and soak them overnight in the refrigerator. Grind $1^{1}/_{3}$ cups of soaked garbanzos in a meat grinder or chop them in a blender without water. Blend the remaining $^{2}/_{3}$ cup of garbanzos with $^{1}/_{2}$ cup cold water until ground fine. Add the garlic, parsley, cumin, and salt, and combine with the ground garbanzos. Drop spoonfuls of mixture into a bowl of bread crumbs and turn them to coat, forming a small ball with your fingers if necessary.

Put them on an ungreased baking pan, cover with foil, and bake at 350° for 15 minutes. Then turn them over and bake for 10 minutes uncovered. Serve hot on pita bread with tahini sauce (recipe below), chopped cucumbers, tomato, lettuce, and green onion. Makes 2 dozen.

Tahini Sauce, Deluxe Version

1 cup sesame seeds
2 tablespoons oil
$^1/_2$ cup water
1 teaspoon salt
$^1/_4$ cup lemon juice

Put all ingredients in a blender and whirl until the seeds are ground fine. A touch of soy sauce may be added or used in place of the lemon juice if you wish. Makes about 1 cup.

Pita
A Middle Eastern flatbread, to serve with falafels.

1 tablespoon dry yeast
$^1/_4$ cup warm water
1 teaspoon salt
$^3/_4$ cup warm water
about $2^1/_2$ cups whole wheat flour

Dissolve the yeast in $^1/_4$ cup water; then add the salt and $^3/_4$ cup water. Add the flour. Turn the dough out on a floured board and knead it until smooth and elastic.

Let it rise in a warm place until double in bulk, turn it out on a floured board, and form it into 12 balls. Roll each into a circle $^{1}/_{4}$ inch thick; place them on a greased baking sheet and let them rise for 15 minutes. Then bake at 500° for 10 minutes. Make sure they don't brown too much. Makes 12.

Garbanzo-Wheat Patties

When combined with any form of wheat, as in falafels and pita, garbanzos supply a high grade of protein to the diet. Here's a main dish that takes advantage of the combination.

1 medium onion, chopped
1 tablespoon oil
2 cups dried garbanzo beans, soaked overnight in water
1 cup cold water
2 cups cooked whole-grain wheat
1 teaspoon salt
1 teaspoon thyme
1 teaspoon sage
2 tablespoons chopped parsley

Sauté the onion in the oil. Blend the garbanzos with the cold water until very fine. Combine them with the cooked wheat, onions, seasonings, and parsley. Form into patties and bake in an ungreased pan, covered, for 30 minutes.

Turn them over, cover, and bake 10 minutes more. Serve with a tomato or mushroom sauce, or you might try the gravy recipe below. Serves 6.

Mock Chicken Gravy

If you soak and freeze them overnight, garbanzo beans can be ground into flour; or you can buy garbanzo flour at a natural-food store. This recipe tastes so much like chicken that we can understand where the nickname chick peas came from.

1 cup oil
2 cups garbanzo flour
5 cups water
$^1/_2$ cup soy sauce
$^1/_2$ teaspoon dill weed
$^1/_2$ teaspoon basil
sea salt
$^1/_4$ cup lemon juice

Heat the oil and stir in the flour with a fork until it's lightly browned. Remove from the heat and cool. Add 2 cups of water and the soy sauce, and place over low heat, cooking and stirring with a whisk until the mixture begins to thicken. Add more water to make smooth gravy. Then add the herbs and salt. Cook until creamy, adding the lemon juice at the very last.

You can serve this over cooked brown rice, beans, bulgar wheat, or any form of pasta. Makes about 6 cups of gravy.

Garbanzo Casserole with Cream Sauce

Here's another main dish you'll enjoy.

1 cup dried garbanzo beans
$^1/_8$ cup soy sauce
$^1/_2$ onion, chopped
1 teaspoon sea salt
pinch of cayenne
2 medium tomatoes, sliced
$^1/_2$ cup grated cheese

Wash the beans thoroughly, and soak them overnight in water to cover. Place them in a pot and cover with water at least an inch above the beans. Add the soy sauce, onion, salt, and cayenne. Cook, covered, for a couple of hours, adding more water as necessary to keep the beans covered. When they are done they should be neither hard nor mushy, but fork-tender.

Put a layer in a greased casserole, cover with a layer of sliced tomatoes and grated cheese, and add the rest of the beans, tomatoes, and cheese. Cover with Whole Wheat Cream Sauce, (see page 181) flavored with onion and bay leaf, and bake at 350° for 25 minutes. Serves 4.

Chick Pea Soup

$1^1/2$ cups dried garbanzo beans
$3^1/2$ cups water
salt to taste
4 cups chicken broth
$^1/4$ cup olive oil
chopped leaves from 1 sprig of mint
$^1/4$ cup chopped parsley
3 teaspoons minced garlic

Soak the peas in the water in the refrigerator overnight; then simmer them in a pot with the salt for $1^1/2$ to 2 hours. Add the chicken broth and heat. Put into a blender the oil, mint, parsley and garlic, and add about $1^1/2$ cups of garbanzos and 1 cup of hot liquid. Blend until smooth. Pour back into the pot and heat to a simmer; do not boil. Serves 6-8.

You may also substitute navy or white beans in this recipe.

Playing With Soybeans

We've had a lot of fun with soybeans. Frankly, we've never really gotten them to behave for us. We cook 'em and cook 'em, and the little rascals stay pretty tough and crunchy. So lately we've taken a new approach. We just forget all about the fact that soybeans are beans. We've begun to threat them like the Chinese and Japanese do — we beat the hell out of them with blenders and hammers, and add them to other things so we won't taste them.

Candidly, we never really liked the taste of soybeans, mild as it is. But we can't deny that they are the finest vegetable-protein food on the face of the planet. Soy protein is great in quality, and there's plenty of it. So here are some of the games that we play with soybeans, and we invite you to join in.

Soy Flour

This is the easiest approach. Just go down to your natural food store, buy a bag of soy flour, and add it to bread recipes, health drinks, and whatever. You'll find soy flour very useful. Just keep it handy so that you'll be reminded to put it in with other foods.

Soy Grits

This is the second easiest approach. These are partially cooked, cracked or coarsely ground soybeans. Buy these at your natural-food store, too. Then just chuck a small amount in with hot cereals, other grains, casseroles, soups, and so on. They tend to take on the flavor of whatever's cooking along with them, and they sure add extra nutritional value.

Sprouting Soybeans

Soak the beans overnight, drain them in the morning, and leave them in a warm place. Flood them with lukewarm water at least *4 or 5 times a day*, draining each time. In 4 to 6 days the sprouts should be 2 to 3 inches long. Then store them in a cool place and use them like any other sprouts (see pages 91-96).

You may find that some beans just won't sprout, and others will ferment or mildew before they sprout. They're either too old or a weird variety. So just don't use that kind any more. Seed beans are best.

Soy Dairy Products

There's a whole range of milk-like products that can be derived from soybeans, even at home. Turn to page 147 for directions and recipes.

Soy Coffee

Roast the soybeans in your oven until they are quite dark, then grind them in your blender or coffee or grain grinder. Use them exactly like coffee. Alternatively, roasted soybeans can be mixed with dried fruits, grains, and chicory.

Trying to Cook Soybeans

Actually, it's not quite so hard if you know a few tricks. Like other beans, soybeans will cook much faster if you soak them first overnight. Always keep them in the refrigerator while soaking, since they ferment easily. To speed up the cooking time even more, soak them overnight *in the freezer*. Defrost in the refrigerator the next day. Then when you get ready to cook them, grease or oil the inside of the pan all the way around the top half to help prevent them from boiling over. Add the beans, cover, and cook several hours until tender, adding extra water if necessary.

Soybean-Rice Loaf

2 cups cooked soybeans
$^3/4$ cup homemade tomato juice
2 eggs
2 tablespoons oil
2 stalks celery, chopped
$^1/4$ green pepper, chopped
1 teaspoon sea salt
$^1/2$ teaspoon sage
2 tablespoons minced parsley
1 cup cooked brown rice

Put all the ingredients except the rice into a blender, and blend until smooth. Mix in the rice and pour into an oiled casserole or loaf pan. Bake at 350° for 45 minutes. Serves 6.

Chinese Soybeans

2 cups cooked soybeans
2 onions, chopped
1 apple, diced
$^1/_4$ cup molasses
1 teaspoon powdered ginger
2 tablespoons soy sauce

Heat the soybeans and add the remaining ingredients, cooking only about 15 minutes so that the onions and apple remain crisp. Serves 4.

Introducing Miso

Although most of us are familiar with soy sauce, we remain unaware of the many other soybean products which can be used for flavoring. One of these is miso, a fermented soybean paste in a highly concentrated form which has been used as an all-purpose seasoning for generations in Japan.

If you find vegetarian fare such as beans, rice, millet, bulgar, or vegetable soups too bland and uninteresting, add a tablespoonful of miso paste dissolved in some hot stock to give a richer look and taste to your dishes. Miso also has excellent nutritional value: it's full of good-quality protein, and it's one of the few vegetarian sources of vitamin B_{12}.

Mexican Soybeans

2 cups cooked soybeans
2 tablespoons chili power, or 1 chopped fresh chili pepper
$^1/_4$ cup tomato ketchup
1 onion, chopped
$^1/_2$ cup grated cheese

Simmer all together until the flavors are well blended. Serves 4.

Soybean Vegetable Stew

1 onion, chopped
$^{1}/_{2}$ green pepper, chopped
1 large carrot, grated
2 stalks celery, sliced
3 tablespoons minced parsley
1 clove garlic, minced
3 tablespoons oil
2 cups cooked soybeans
3 tomatoes, chopped
1 teaspoon basil
$^{1}/_{2}$ teaspoon thyme
1 teaspoon sea salt

Sauté all the vegetables except the soybeans and the tomatoes in the oil. Whirl the soybeans and tomatoes in a blender for a few seconds. Mix them with the sautéed vegetables and seasonings, and simmer a few minutes until the flavors are blended.

The mixture can also be poured into a casserole, adding a bit of stock if too dry, and topped with wheat germ or bread crumbs and baked for 20 minutes at 350°. Serves 4.

Peppers Stuffed with Soy Grits

4 large bell peppers
1 small onion, minced
1 clove garlic, minced
2 tablespoons oil
1 cup soy grits
1 cup stock or water
1 teaspoon summer savory
$^{1}/_{2}$ teaspoon basil
1 teaspoon sea salt
$^{1}/_{2}$ cup cooked brown rice

Cut the tops off the peppers and scoop out the seeds. Blanch them for a few minutes in some boiling water. Sauté the onion and garlic in the oil. Cook the soy grits in the stock or water for 5 minutes; then add the onion, garlic, herbs, salt and rice. Fill the peppers and place them in a casserole with a small amount of water or stock. Bake at 350° for 35 to 40 minutes. Serves 4.

Soybean Spread

1 cup cooked soybeans
$^1/_4$ cup minced onion
$^1/_4$ cup minced green pepper
2 tablespoons minced parsley
$^1/_2$ teaspoon cumin
$^1/_2$ teaspoon oregano
$^1/_2$ teaspoon garlic salt
$^1/_2$ cup yogurt

Blend all the ingredients in a blender and spread on crackers or celery. Try dill, caraway, or other seasonings for variety. Makes about 2 cups.

What would we do without dairy foods? There isn't a chapter in this book that doesn't include eggs, milk or cheese in at least some of the recipes. The reason is simple: dairy foods not only will accommodate the flavors of many other kinds of foods, but provide excellent-quality protein that makes up for the protein deficiencies in grains, vegetables, beans, and seeds. Not to mention their wonderful calcium and vitamins!

We love meals based on dairy foods and vegetables. Why not break the meat routine with this combination at least once a week? Somehow, eating these lighter foods can make your whole life more ebullient. Try it and see if we're not right.

Now, eggs and cheese, and that all-time favorite yogurt, can wind up being pretty expensive, especially if you start using them as much as we do.

EGGS MILK & CHEESE

The answer is, make (or in the case of eggs, produce) them at home! We're going to tell you how.

Eggs, The Nearly Perfect Protein

As Frances Moore Lappé explains in *Diet for a Small Planet*, eggs contain the most perfect protein that Mother Nature has to offer. No other food has a better balance of the eight essential amino acids for the human body. Even at 15¢ apiece or more, eggs are a good buy. Plan by all means to include some in your 99¢ a meal menu.

Know how to tell a fresh egg from an old one? Hard-boiled from uncooked? How to raise some quiet egg producers?

- Fresh eggs won't balance on either end because the yolk is in the center. A stale egg has the yolk at one end, and will balance.
- Hard-boiled eggs will spin smoothly, since their contents are solid; raw eggs have an erratic spin due to their shifting fluid innards.
- Quail eggs are delicious, and so are quails. You can raise these quiet little pets for eggs and food in any small back yard without disturbing the neighbors.

If you have some outdoor space available and tolerant neighbors, why not raise regular chickens? They are easy to care for, will eat all your table scraps, and produce nice fresh eggs free of artificial hormones. To get your own egg factory going, just buy a few layers or pullets, feed them grain and leftovers such as aging greens and fruit, let them roost in the trees, and they'll be so happy they'll lay your eggs wherever you set up a nest. All you need for that is a box with some straw in it.

What can you do with eggs? Everybody knows what to do with them at breakfast time, so we're going to give you some recipes that are great for lunch or dinner.

Egg-Tomato Curry

1 cup raw brown rice
2 onions, chopped
2 cloves garlic, minced
3 tablespoons butter or oil
$2^{1}/_{2}$ teaspoons curry powder
5 large ripe tomatoes, chopped
1 teaspoon sea salt
2 cups stock
1 teaspoon honey
2 tablespoons flour
6 hard-boiled eggs

Cook the rice. Sauté the onion and garlic in the butter or oil until tender. Stir in the curry powder and cook 3 minutes. Add the chopped tomatoes, salt, stock, honey, and flour. Stir over low heat until the sauce is thick. Slice the hard-boiled eggs and gently fold them into the sauce. Heat the sauce gently and serve it over the rice. Serves 4.

Egg Bonanza Casserole

$^{1}/_{2}$ cup chopped onion
$^{1}/_{4}$ cup butter or oil
2 chicken bouillon cubes

1 teaspoon dry mustard
$^1/_2$ teaspoon basil
$^1/_4$ teaspoon thyme
1 teaspoon sea salt
pepper to taste
$^1/_3$ cup flour
$2^1/_2$ cups milk
1 teaspoon prepared horseradish
1 tablespoon minced chives
2 tablespoons chopped parsley
5 medium potatoes, cooked and sliced
6 hard-boiled eggs, sliced
$^1/_4$ cup grated cheddar cheese

Sauté the onion in the butter until soft. Add the bouillon cubes, mustard, herbs, salt, and pepper. Blend in the flour; then stir in the milk and cook, stirring constantly, until the sauce boils and thickens. Add the horseradish, chives, and parsley.

Put a layer of potatoes in a greased 2-quart baking dish and cover them with a layer of sliced eggs and half the sauce. Repeat the layers and sprinkle the top with cheese. Bake at 350° for about 30 minutes. Serves 6.

Cheesy Egg-Noodle Bake

1 cup noodles
4 hard-boiled eggs, sliced
1 cup homemade cottage cheese
1 cup shredded jack cheese
1 teaspoon salt
1 tablespoon minced onion
$^3/_4$ teaspoon Italian seasoning, or a blend of basil, oregano, rosemary, and bay leaf
$1^1/_2$ cups milk, scalded

Cook the noodles until tender; drain, rinse, and cool. Put a layer of noodles in a buttered 2-quart casserole, cover them with half of the eggs, half of the cottage cheese, dropped by spoonfuls, half of the jack cheese, and half of the seasonings mixed with the onion. Repeat the layers. Pour the scalded milk over all and bake at 350° for 45 minutes. Serves 6.

Hearty Macaroni Salad

1 cup macaroni, preferably small
4 hard-boiled eggs, cut in sixths
1 can tuna
1 cup celery, chopped
$^1/_2$ cup onion, chopped
1 tablespoon chopped parsley
1 teaspoon sea salt
$^2/_3$ cup mayonnaise

Cook the macaroni until tender; drain, rinse, and cool. Reserve one egg cut in sixths; cut the remaining eggs in half horizontally. Combine the tuna, eggs, celery, onion, parsley, and salt in a large bowl. Stir in the macaroni and blend in the mayonnaise. Chill thoroughly before serving and garnish with the reserved egg sections. Serves 6.

The Wild Duck

Ruth and I were gently floating down one of the channels of the San Joaquin River. The day was peaceful and warm, the banks of the levees were festooned with willows and blackberries in full leaf, and we were enjoying a certain nirvana that seems to be associated with life on the water. I casually gazed ahead and noticed a duck sitting on a floating plank. As we slowly approached, the duck quacked, waddled across the plank, jumped in the water, and swam away.

She left a generous token of her love of humanity on the plank — a warm, newly laid egg. As we drifted by, I stuck out my hand and scooped the egg off the plank, tucking it in my shirt pocket.

Ruth turned to me with a quizzical expression. "Why is it, Bill, that your whole life seems to be just a long drift down a river where you simply reach out your hand and pick up free food for tomorrow's breakfast?"

"I don't know," I grinned; "just unlucky I guess."

Egg and Tomato Rarebit

6 firm ripe tomatoes
6 eggs
garlic salt and pepper
1 tablespoon melted butter
2 tablespoons bread crumbs
1 teaspoon chopped parsley
$^1/_2$ teaspoon basil
$1^1/_2$ cups Whole-Wheat Cream Sauce (see page 181)
$^1/_2$ cup grated cheddar cheese
$^1/_4$ teaspoon dry mustard
6 slices whole-wheat toast

Scoop out the center of the tomatoes and drain. Break an egg into each tomato cup. Place the tomatoes in a buttered baking dish and sprinkle them with garlic salt and pepper. Combine the butter, bread crumbs, parsley, and basil, and sprinkle on the eggs. Bake for 30 minutes at 300°.

Meanwhile, combine the white sauce, cheese, and mustard in a saucepan, and stir until the cheese is melted. Place each baked tomato and egg on a slice of toast and pour the cheese sauce over it. Serves 6.

Eggs Goldenrod

Hardboil six eggs, peel and slice lengthwise. Remove yolks (save one) and mash with mayonnaise, a bit of salt and cayenne. Replace the mixture in eggs and sprinkle with grated yolk. A simple dish that makes a delicious and fairly inexpensive canapé or picnic item. Could even be a main protein source with a hearty soup and salad.

Herb Omelet

3 eggs
3 tablespoons water
$^1/_2$ teaspoon salt
$^1/_4$ teaspoon pepper
1 tablespoon chopped chives
$^1/_4$ teaspoon each basil, thyme, oregano, and parsley
1 tablespoon butter

Mix the eggs, water, salt, pepper, and any or all of the above herbs according to your liking. Heat the butter in a skillet just hot enough to sizzle a drop of water. Pour in the egg mixture and reduce the heat slightly.

As the mixture at the edges thickens, draw these portions with a fork toward the center so that the uncooked portions flow to the bottom. Tilt the skillet to hasten the flow of uncooked egg, and shake the skillet to keep the omelet sliding freely. When the eggs are set, roll the omelet out onto a serving plate. Serves 1 prodigiously; 2 handsomely.

Huevos Rancheros

This is the classic Mexican egg dish which you'll find offered in every Latino restaurant. It can be prepared in many ways but we like this one best.

Chop a large onion, three cloves of garlic, 2 large tomatoes, as many chopped Jalapeño peppers as you can handle and sauté in olive oil. Add 2 cups tomato juice and simmer slowly until thickened. Season to taste with sugar, salt and pepper.

Break eggs gently (two per person) into simmering sauce and poach to order. Use a spatula to serve eggs on top of heated and buttered tortillas. Top with more sauce if desired and sprinkle with fresh chopped cilantro and Parmesan. Serve extra tortillas on the side for a filling and satisfying breakfast.

Milk,
Dry And Goat's

We were doing a lot of traveling at one time, and fluid milk was inconvenient to carry, so we bought a 50-pound bag of dry skim milk to take along. That was over three years ago and we're just finishing up our 50 pounds now. There's no question that dry skim milk is the way to go. We think that the fluid milk sold in stores is a bad deal because you're paying for the expensive packaging of a product that's mainly water.

Remember that instant milk powder is fine when you want to mix up some for drinking, but non-instant must be used in cooking and making yogurt and cheese. Also, we do indulge in whole milk for these last two.

In Mexico we discovered that the peasant "cow" is a goat. Goats provide excellent milk and are easier and cheaper to raise than cows. If you have a small spread in the country, goats will keep down the weeds and you won't have to buy much feed. Also, goat's milk cheese is delicious and easy to make.

Recipes using milk of one form or another are scattered throughout this book, reflecting milk's matchless value as an all-purpose food. Here we do want to share with you two recipes for healthy, cheap versions of classic, rich dairy desserts, and a third recipe for your own health-drink mix using powdered milk.

Low-Cal Vanilla Ice Cream

$1^1/2$ cups skim-milk powder
3 cups water
$^2/3$ cup honey
1 envelope unflavored gelatin
3 eggs, separated
1 tablespoon vanilla

Combine the skim-milk powder and water in a blender with the honey, and place it in the top of a double boiler over hot water. Mix the gelatin with $^1/4$ cup water, and stir into the hot milk mixture. Beat the egg yolks and stir in a little of the hot milk, then pour them into the remaining milk mixture and stir over boiling water until the mixture coats the spoon.

Remove from the heat and add the vanilla. Allow to cool; then pour into refrigerator trays and freeze. Just before serving, beat the egg whites and the frozen mixture together in a large bowl until fluffy. Any leftover ice cream can be rebeaten each time before serving. Makes about 1 quart.

Poor Man's Bavarian Pudding

1 envelope unflavored gelatin
$^1/2$ cup skim-milk powder, blended with $1^1/2$ cups water
2 egg yolks
$^1/4$ cup honey
pinch of salt
1 teaspoon vanilla
2 egg whites

Soften the gelatin in the milk in the top of a double boiler. Beat the egg yolks with the honey and salt, and add them to the milk. Cook the mixture over hot water or very low heat, stirring constantly, until it coats the spoon. Cool and add the vanilla.

Beat the egg whites until stiff, fold them into the pudding, and pour it into a mold rinsed in cold water. Chill until firm. This may be served with any kind of fresh or stewed fruit if desired. Serves 4.

Your Own Health-Drink Mix

Health-food stores (as distinguished from natural-food stores) are not above taking advantage of the hapless consumer. In fact, they can be the worst offenders, since they often have a holier-than-thou attitude to boot. For example, most of them sell prepared health-drink mixes that are extravagantly overpriced.

The solution, as usual, is make your own! Here's a close copy of a health-drink mix.

10 ounces soy flour or soy isolate
2 ounces lecithin in granular form
1 ounce brewer's yeast
2 ounces milk powder prepared by the spray process
1 ounce flavoring — carob, vanilla, or whatever you like (quantity may be adjusted to suit your taste). Your cost is about $1/6$ of the retail.

Just put all the ingredients (which are dry) into a container, put on the lid, and shake. Now you can make a number of blender drinks in nothing flat. Put milk or fruit juice in your blender container, add a few tablespoons of your homemade health drink mix, and blend. That's all there is to it!

Pineapple Upside Down Cake
(To go with your drink)

$^1/_2$ cup brown sugar
$^3/_4$ cup whole-wheat flour
1 teaspoon baking powder
$^1/_2$ teaspoon salt
1 egg
$^1/_3$ cup milk
$^1/_2$ teaspoon vanilla
$^1/_2$ teaspoon lemon extract

Mix the above ingredients together to make a cake batter. Melt $^3/_4$ cup brown sugar and 3 tablespoons butter in pan. Add six small pineapple slices. Pour in cake batter and bake at 350° until a toothpick comes out clean.

Homemade Cheese & Yogurt

As you have probably noticed, cheese and yogurt are used in many, many recipes throughout this book. Rather than add still more recipes for using them here, we decided to give you some tips on cutting costs by making your own cheese and yogurt at home.

But first, we want to make special mention of one of the best cheese dishes we know. Undoubtedly you know it too: the open-faced broiled cheese sandwich. Never underestimate this little beauty. Purists like it absolutely straight — just a slice of cheese on bread, placed under the broiler to melt. If you want to gild the lily, make it on rye bread and slice a few pimento-stuffed green olives over it. Or, for a whole meal, try this:

Your Own Cottage Cheese

This is so simple, you'll wonder why you never tried it before:

1 quart whole milk
2 tablespoons lemon juice

Heat the milk just to scalding; do not boil. Remove from the heat and add the lemon juice. Cover and let it sit on the sink for several hours at room temperature. Now pour the mixture through a strainer or colander which has been lined with two thicknesses of cheesecloth and placed over a bowl.

You may refrigerate the liquid or whey which drips through and use it to mix with non-instant milk powder for making yogurt. Allow the cheese mixture to drain for several hours or until it's dry.

If you want to make a harder cheese, put the mixture between two boards and apply pressure. The combination of squeezing and drying will give you a more characteristic cheese. You can add some sea salt if you wish and then refrigerate. Could anything be easier?

Last year we were in Mendocino County, California, where we met a charming couple, the Sinclairs of Little River. Judy makes her own goat's milk cheese, and what they don't eat, she sells. It's so simple and yet so good. The method is the same as for cottage cheese, except that you only need about a teaspoonful of lemon juice to each quart of scalded goat's milk.

One of Judy's great inventions is green onion cheese. All you do is chop up some green onions or scallions and add them to the curdled milk just before you squeeze it out.

Vegetable Grinder Sandwich with Cheese

On slices of whole-wheat bread lay the following raw vegetables sliced thinly: onion, zucchini, green pepper, mushrooms, avocado, and tomato. Over the top lay a thin slice of cheese, and place the sandwich under the broiler until the cheese has melted. A great lunch for everybody!

Comment: Making your own sandwiches makes good sense. Years ago, as a restaurant consultant, I learned that about 80% of what you pay for food is overhead and profit. Typically, the food cost in a ten dollar meal is about $2.

Your Own Yogurt

One of the best arguments for making your own yogurt is that the commercial varieties contain many unnecessary additives that you are better off without. These can include emulsifiers, starches, carrageenan, guar gum, cellulose, and worst of all, sugar and artificial flavorings. When you make yogurt yourself, you know exactly what went into it; and all you really need is milk and a starter.

The latter can be from a good-quality yogurt you purchased at a natural-food store or some left over from your last batch. Here are the proportions:

1 cup whole milk
2 tablespoons starter
1 cup warm water
1 cup non-instant milk powder
2 cups warm water

Put the first 3 ingredients into your blender and whirl. Gradually add the non-instant milk powder and the remaining warm water. Pour into several small glass jars or one large glass container, cover, and keep at 110° for several hours until you have yogurt. The time it takes varies according to the weather. Makes about 1 quart.

There are various methods you can use to maintain the proper temperature. A regular yogurt maker is of course ideal. You can also set the jars on a food warmer or hot tray, or set them inside a down-filled sleeping bag. You can set your oven at its lowest possible setting, below 200°, and turn it off if it gets too warm. Or simply set the yogurt mixture in small jars inside a larger container and fill this with warm water, adding more hot water from time to time. Other naturally warm areas such as radiators, pilot lights on stove tops, and hot water heaters will work as well.

The longer it sets, the tarter your yogurt will become. Once it's firm, refrigerate it and plan to use it within a week, at which time you can start a fresh batch.

You can flavor your own yogurt with honey, fresh fruits, carob, or molasses, or dried fruits, nuts, and seeds. Yogurt made with the above ingredients will cost you only 40 cents a pint, whereas plain commercial yogurt sells for around $1.40 or more in most markets — just another big argument in favor of the do-it-yourself policy.

Yogurt Smoothie

Whirl your yogurt in the blender with some sliced bananas, pears, apricots, peaches, or any combination of fruits in season. Sweeten with a tablespoonful of honey if desired.

To this you can add other healthful ingredients like wheat germ, brewer's yeast, lecithin, powdered milk, or sunflower seeds to provide a complete breakfast or lunch that will satisfy your hunger for hours.

Kefir

Kefir is a cultured milk product similar to yogurt, except that it's thinner and uses a different culture. To make your own, simply add a tablespoon of store-bought kefir to a quart of skim milk which has been scalded and cooled to 100-110°. Put it in a warm place to make the transition, just as you would do with yogurt.

Yogurt Options

In addition to the yogurt suggestions which we've retained from the previous edition, here are some quick and easy applications of this homemade, low-cost, healthful and versatile dairy item.

- Mix a pinch of salt, a dash of lemon juice and about six tablespoons of blue cheese or Roquefort to a cup of yogurt. Mix well and refrigerate. Wonderful with crisp romaine.
- Whirl some in your blender with additions like vanilla and honey, maple syrup, or cherry juice. Make a fine topping for almost any dessert.
- Thicken yogurt by adding some homemade mayonnaise. Then blend in onions, red onions, a clove of garlic, fresh basil, dash of soy, cayenne and lemon juice. Makes a terrific dip or dressing. Try some over freshly baked potatoes.
- Smoothies via the blender are made of yogurt, soy milk and flavor additions such as almonds, walnuts, oranges, strawberries, apricots, peaches or dates. To thicken, add a little rice flour.
- For sherbet, freeze a pint of yogurt with two cups of crushed fresh fruit. A sensational taste from very ripe papaya.

Your Soybean Dairy

Many people aren't aware that a whole range of milk-like products can be derived from the soybean, even at home. Their nutritional value if excellent, is not quite comparable to that of cow's milk.

Soy Milk

Soak 1 cup soybeans overnight in the refrigerator. Liquefy in the blender with 3 cups of water. Heat the mixture to a boil in a heavy pot (oil the top so it won't boil over) and then simmer over low heat for 20 minutes. Strain through a clean cloth (cheese cloth or a diaper is ideal) placed in a colander or strainer. Add a pinch of salt and sweeten the milk if desired. The pulp remaining in the colander may be used to add to soyburger patties or other recipes calling for mashed soybeans.

Soy milk can be substituted for regular milk in blender drinks, cream sauces, puddings or soups.

Tofu

Finally, familiar to some but unknown to many is tofu — bean cake or curd — also sometimes called soy cheese. If you haven't seen it yet, look for it in natural or co-op food stores, or in Chinese markets. It resembles a firm custard with a creamy white color and a very delicate flavor.

Tofu can be used in many ways; most often it's added to dishes to provide protein and bulk. Cooking with tofu is one good way to create healthful, low-cost meals, since tofu contains good amounts of fairly good quality protein (though it does not rate as high as cow's milk).

Current Comment

Tofu has gone big-time since the previous edition of this book appeared. It can be purchased in many places including the big markets. Also, it has been added to the menus of many restaurants. As meat and milk prices continue to rise, it's a sure bet that soy, tofu, and all the variations will become even more popular... and easy on your budget.

Here's how to make tofu at home.

Your Own Tofu

Boil some soy milk for about 5 minutes and add a small amount (it varies with the conditions) of either magnesium sulfate (Epsom salts) or calcium sulfate. Lemon juice or vinegar also works.

The addition of these substances causes the milk to separate into curds and whey, just as though you were making cheese. Ladle the curds into a cloth-lined strainer or perforated box and press out the moisture with a weighted lid. In a few minutes it will become firm and ready to use. Just chill it in cold water and slice.

Or, you can make tofu from soy flour, if you haven't got any soybeans on hand.

Easy Tofu

1^1/2 cups soy flour
cold water as needed
4^1/2 cups boiling water
6 tablespoons lemon juice

Add enough cold water to the soy flour to make a paste. Beat it until airy. Add the boiling water and cook 5 minutes. Remove the mixture from the heat and add the lemon juice. Curds will form as it cools. Strain it through a cheesecloth and refrigerate it in a plastic bag.

Observation

This is an appropriate place to discuss the rising conscious-ness concerning food that is so evident these days.

Tofu is a good example of the positive steps being made to create a more healthful and humanitarian world. Instead of raising animals for slaughter we are finding more reasons to raise organic veggies such as soy beans.

Could this nutritional transformation be a part of what Teilhard de Chardin called The Metamorphosis of Man? We think so and there's other evidence including the increasing awareness and action relating to our mutual environment.

Let's take a look at some other evidence related to food.

More people than ever are planting home gardens. This is an indication of self-reliance, a most worthy goal. There are many individuals and groups striving to preserve original plants by saving seeds and cuttings. There are many advances being made in the improvement of plant life through genetic research. The alternatives to chemicals are already in action; organic farms are rapidly expanding while giant vacuums take care of bugs. Culinary experts appearing in the print and electronic media are showing us both new and old ways to obtain the best taste and top nutrition simultaneously. Great interest in improved food is being generated by high-profile chefs. Their restaurants are becoming the showplaces of elegant dishes combining appearance, taste and health values. Globally there are still food problems. However, there is more agrarian research underway than ever before.

In summary, there is an abundance of evidence to warrant high hopes where good food at a fair price is concerned.

Tofu and Eggs

Slice tofu like bacon. Fry it lightly in butter, combine it with fried or scrambled eggs, garnish with parsley, and serve. This makes a great breakfast without all the chemicals in bacon.

Vegetable Soup with Tofu

Make your favorite vegetable soup recipe (see pages 58 through 64) and add cubes of tofu during the last 10 minutes. Heat well and serve. Tofu goes well with any kind of soup or stew dish.

Tofu-Vegetable Medley

Sauté some sliced celery, mushrooms, green onions, and whole peas in butter or oil until almost tender. Thicken with cornstarch and boiling water or stock, and add soy sauce or miso to taste.

Cut up of tofu in cubes and add it to the vegetables, stirring gently until the mixture has heated through. Serve over brown rice.

Tofuburgers!

Combine the desired quantity of tofu (well pressed) with chopped onions, chopped garlic, grated carrots, and chopped green peppers. Form it into patties and fry them in $^1/_2$ inch of hot soy oil until they become light and start to float.

These crisp golden delights are fine as is, with soy sauce or ketchup, or in a bun with all the hamburger trimmings.

Tofu, Banana, and Peanut Butter Spread

Mix 12 ounces of tofu with 2 mashed bananas and $^3/_4$ cup of natural, unadorned peanut butter. Add a bit of lemon juice and some honey or molasses if you wish. Use a blender or a large wooden spoon to mix all the ingredients well.

This spread is great as a topping for whole-wheat bread to satisfy hungry children, as a topping for hot cereal, or as a snack with crisp sesame crackers. Keep a bowl in your refrigerator for those moments when you need a nutritious pickup.

We've been staying away from hamburger lately, cheap though it may be. Too often it's padded with extra fat and fillers, and full of chemical colorings, pesticides, and preservatives. It's gotten so we're not sure what's in the stuff any more.

Now, fish and chicken are another story. Catch your own fish, and raise your own hormone-free chickens, and you're in business. You'll never get tired of their delicate flavors, which make them compatible with so many delectable food combinations. You'll feel better, too, sticking to lighter, less fatty entrées like these.

Chicken is so popular all around the world that we doubt anyone is short on favorite chicken recipes. For that reason we've included just a few. There are lots of fish recipes, though, for those who need help with some more imaginative ways to fix fish of all kinds.

FISH & FOWL

Fish,
Free and Otherwise

One of the great advantages to fish is that it's a food you can often catch yourself. During the Great Depression in the thirties many Americans not only survived but thrived on a diet of fresh fish.

Acquire a length of gill net at a fisherman's supply store. Simply stretch the net in any likely underwater spot and then go on about your business. Small fish can swim right through the net, but big ones get caught. When they try to back out they are trapped by their gills. So all you have to do is pull up the net once in a while and take off your fresh breakfast, lunch or dinner.

Set lines are a trick I learned from some resourceful men who lived in fish shanties in San Pedro Harbor, California, in the mid-thirties. Attach a hook to a piece of fish line. Attach the free end to any kind of float — a piece of wood, an empty jug, or whatever. Attach a stronger line to the float with any kind of anchor on the other end — a rock or a piece of scrap metal, for example. Now bait the hook and toss the whole assembly into the water, making sure that the hook doesn't drag on the bottom. You may want to set several of these lines at once. Again, sit down with a good book and the fish will catch themselves.

Catfish Gumbo

The legendary catfish: it's easy to catch, delicious, and probably one of the cheapest high-quality foods you can obtain anywhere. If you don't live in catfish country, though, you can make this gumbo with almost any other kind of fish as well.

1 pound skinned catfish fillets
$^1/_2$ cup celery, chopped
$^1/_2$ cup green pepper, chopped
$^1/_2$ cup onion, chopped
1 clove garlic, minced
$^1/_4$ cup oil
2 beef bouillon cubes
2 cups boiling water
1 pound fresh tomatoes, chopped
1 cup fresh okra, sliced
2 teaspoons salt
pepper to taste
$^1/_2$ teaspoon thyme
1 bay leaf
dash hot pepper sauce
$1^1/_2$ cups hot cooked rice

Cut the fish into 1-inch pieces. Sauté the celery, green pepper, onion, and garlic in the oil until tender. Add the bouillon cubes dissolved in the water, the tomatoes, okra and seasonings. Cover and simmer for 15 minutes. Add the fish. Cover and simmer for 30 minutes more, or until the fish flakes easily with a fork. Remove the bay leaf. Place $^1/_4$ cup rice in each of 6 soup bowls and fill with gumbo. Serves 6.

In my files I have a tabloid story about a man who was laid off from his factory job and moved his family onto a houseboat. His task was to catch 2 or 3 catfish per day to keep food on the table. Evidently he was able to do it and contended that living in the Mississippi Delta was far better than the old 8 to 5. I heartily agree.

Country Fried Catfish

Fried catfish — the very words elicit a vision of misty morning on some romantic river. With it, of course, hush puppies or cornbread. Mmmmm! What a gourmet treat for peanut money and effort! This recipe is designed for that happy day when you have lots of friends and relatives around to help you enjoy your river-rat life.

2 eggs, beaten
$^1/_4$ cup milk
$1^1/_2$ teaspoons sea salt
$^1/_4$ teaspoon pepper
2 cups whole-wheat flour
2 cups bread crumbs
25 skinned catfish
oil for frying

Combine the eggs, milk, salt, and pepper. Combine the flour and bread crumbs. Dip the fish in the egg mixture and roll it in the flour and crumbs. Fry it in oil heated to 350° for 3 to 5 minutes, or until the fish flakes easily with a fork. Drain on absorbent paper. Feeds 25!

Squid with Rice

Many people are squeamish about squid, but do try it. It's too good and cheap to pass up.

3 tablespoons minced green onions
2 cloves garlic, minced
$^1/_4$ cup minced parsley
2 tablespoons butter
2 pounds squid, cleaned and sliced in rings

1 cup raw brown rice, cooked preferably in fish stock
grated Parmesan cheese

Sauté the vegetables in the butter until soft. Raise the heat and sauté the squid for 4 or 5 minutes. Serve with the cooked rice and sprinkle with the Parmesan cheese. Serves 6.

Kebabs

This recipe works for any kind of fish including squid. Make up a marinade of fresh lemon juice, olive oil, pepper, hot sauce and your favorite spices — we suggest that oregano be included. Toss in 2-inch pieces of fish and while they are absorbing a delicious flavor, build a campfire on the beach. Cut some sweet-wood twigs for skewers. Then chop an onion and a green pepper into chunks and skewer them in alternate sequence with the fish. Broil slowly, turning often, over the coals. We'll guarantee that this outdoor meal will outclass any restaurant you'll find.

Fish Cakes

Here's a good way to use up that leftover cooked fish and stale bread.

2 slices bread
1 cup milk
3 cups cooked fish, flaked
1 egg, beaten
$1/4$ cup parsley, minced
$1/2$ teaspoon sea salt
$1/4$ teaspoon pepper
$1/4$ teaspoon nutmeg
3 tablespoons butter
3 tablespoons oil

Soak the bread in the milk until soft. Combine with the fish, beaten egg, parsley, and seasonings. Form into cakes and brown them on each side in the butter and oil until heated through. Serves 6.

Halibut Chowder

Halibut is a bottom fish easily caught by anyone who puts his bait on the line about a foot above the sinker. I recall as a young fisherman working out of San Pedro that when nothing else was biting, the halibut were. The following recipe would of course be suitable for almost any other fish of a similar texture.

1 clove garlic, minced
$^1/_2$ cup onion, chopped
$^3/_4$ cup green pepper, minced
3 tablespoons olive oil
4 medium tomatoes, chopped
1 cup tomato sauce
$^1/_2$ cup sliced ripe olives
1 bay leaf, crumbled
$^1/_2$ teaspoon oregano
1 teaspoon salt
1 cup water
1 pound halibut cut in 1-inch pieces

Sauté the garlic, onion, and green pepper in the oil until tender. Add the tomatoes, tomato sauce, olives, herbs, and salt. Cover and cook over low heat for 45 minutes. Add the water and cook 10 minutes longer. Add the fish and cook 5 to 10 minutes, or until it flakes easily with a fork. Serves 6.

Saving Fish

Fish deteriorates rapidly so here are some ways to save it. Cook it and refrigerate. Once cooked it will be suitable for fishwiches, salads, and as add-ons for soups and salads.

If you have lots, take it to a professional smoker. Often they will take a percentage of the smoked output as their pay. Alternatively, brush the fish chunks with natural smoke flavor and place on a grill over a slow fire of sweet green wood. Refrigerate what you don't eat.

Sun dry it as natives do all over the world. The thinner you slice it, the faster it will dry.

Poached White Fish in Dill Sauce

Know anyone who doesn't like fish? Try this on them. You can use any white, unoily fish such as haddock, cod, halibut, flounder, or sole; just make sure it's very fresh.

3 tablespoons butter or oil
3 tablespoons whole-wheat pastry flour
2 cups milk
1 teaspoon salt
1 teaspoon dried dill, or about 3 tablespoons fresh
1-1$^1/_2$ pounds fish fillets

Put the butter, flour, milk and salt in a blender and whirl. Pour the mixture into a heavy 3-quart pot and whisk or stir it constantly over medium heat until it thickens. When it boils, turn down the heat, add the dill, and simmer for a few minutes.

Cut up the fish in 1-inch cubes and gently mix it into the sauce. Cover the pan and let the fish poach gently for 5 or 6 minutes, never letting the sauce boil. The fish should flake easily when done, but be careful not to let it overcook. Serves 6.

Scalloped Fish and Potatoes

1^1/2 pounds any firm fish
^{2}/3 cup flour
2 teaspoons sea salt
pepper to taste
6 cups thinly sliced raw potatoes
2 cups thinly sliced onions
^{1}/4 cup butter
3 cups hot milk
paprika

Cut the fish into ^{1}/2-inch slices. Combine the flour with salt and pepper. Spread a third of the potato slices and half of the onion and fish slices in a greased 3-quart casserole. Sprinkle with half of the flour and dot with half of the butter.

Repeat the layers, using the remaining third of the potatoes for the top. Pour the milk over the casserole and sprinkle it with paprika. Cover the casserole with aluminum foil and bake at 375° for 1 hour. Serves 6-8.

Clam & Corn Chowder

3 slices bacon
1 cup chopped onion
2 cups diced raw potatoes
1 cup clam liquid or water
1^1/2 cups fresh corn kernels
3 cups milk made with skim-milk powder
2 tablespoons flour
1 tablespoon butter
1 teaspoon celery salt
1 teaspoon salt
dash of pepper
1 cup minced clams

Fry the bacon until it's almost done; add the onion and cook until tender. Add the potatoes and clam liquid or water. Cover and simmer gently until the potatoes are tender. Add the corn and milk.

Blend the flour and butter, and stir them into the chowder. Cook slowly until the mixture thickens, stirring constantly. Add the seasonings and clams, and simmer 5 minutes. Serve hot and pass the crackers. Serves 6.

One-Pot Clam Chowder

$^{1}/_{4}$ pound salt pork, diced
1 large onion, sliced
2 medium carrots, diced
2 celery stalks, chopped
$^{1}/_{2}$ green pepper, diced
1 cup chopped fresh tomatoes
3 cups water
$^{1}/_{4}$ teaspoon freshly ground pepper
1 teaspoon sea salt
$^{1}/_{2}$ teaspoon thyme
$^{1}/_{2}$ teaspoon oregano
1 cup whole-wheat or soy elbow macaroni
1 can minced clams (6$^{1}/_{2}$ ounces), or 1 cup fresh minced clams

In a heavy pot sauté the diced salt pork until crisp and remove it from the pan with a slotted spoon. Sauté the onion, carrots, celery, and green pepper in the drippings, adding a little oil if necessary.

When the vegetables are just crisp-tender, add the tomatoes, water, seasonings, and macaroni. Bring to a boil, stirring frequently. Reduce the heat, cover, and simmer until the macaroni is almost tender, about 10 to 12 minutes. Add the clams with their juice and continue simmering until the macaroni is tender. Serves 6.

Clambake Anyone?

Clams are one of the easiest free foods to acquire which is why we're offering a selection of ways to prepare them. They grow spontaneously in both fresh and salt water. All you need is a shovel or, lacking that, use your hands.

Incidentally, they make good bait for your fish hooks if you have any left over.

Fisherman's Luck

Living on our boat often produced unexpected bonanzas, such as finding a trap full of crayfish. If you have some, fine; if not, use any salt- or fresh-water fish, boned and cut into chunks, for a delicious fish stir-fry.

Chop a large stalk of celery and start sautéing it in your well-oiled wok (or heavy frying pan). Add a chopped onion slightly above the celery. Place a chopped green pepper in the same general area, and cook a few minutes. When these are just barely tender, add a cup of cooked rice and plenty of soy sauce or miso, and toss in the pieces of fish. Stir until the fish is just delicately cooked. Serve hot with crisp Chinese chow mein noodles.

With a spot of hot tea you have a feast that's satisfying and non-fattening!

California Delta Paella

Life in the Sacramento River Delta aboard The Flying Goose is not all that bad when you can enjoy some of the fresh foods that abound in the region.

$^{1}/_{2}$ pound green beans
1 cup fresh shelled peas
2 onions, peeled
6 tablespoons oil
2 tablespoons minced parsley

3 cloves garlic, minced
2 green peppers, chopped
1 red hot pepper, seeded and chopped
$1^1/2$ cups raw brown rice
4-6 large tomatoes, peeled and chopped
$1/8$ teaspoon saffron, optional
salt and pepper
2 cups water
2 bay leaves
12 crayfish
$1^1/2$ quarts cleaned mussels
1 large chorizo (Mexican) sausage, sliced
2 tablespoons oil

Bring a large pan of salted water to a boil and add the beans, the peas, and 1 whole peeled onion. Cook 15 minutes. Drain the vegetables and put them aside, saving the cooking liquid. Preheat the oven to 400°.

Heat 6 tablespoons of oil in your largest iron skillet and add the second onion, chopped, along with the parsley and garlic. Sauté a few minutes; add the green and red peppers, and cook a few minutes longer. Add the rice and stir it for a few minutes. Reboil the vegetable cooking liquid and add enough of it to cover the rice by about an inch. Add the tomatoes, saffron, peas, beans, and salt and pepper. Cover the skillet and place it in the oven for 40 minutes.

Meanwhile, heat 2 cups of water in a saucepan with the bay leaves. When it boils, add the crayfish and cook them over high heat for 10 minutes. Remove them from the water.

Scrub the mussels under running water; then place them in the boiling liquid and cook for about 8 to 10 minutes. Remove the pan from the heat and lift the mussels out, discarding any that haven't opened. Brown the sausage in 2 tablespoons of oil until it's cooked through. Serve the rice in a large tureen or bowl garnished with the shellfish and sausage. Makes a magnificent meal for 6 to 8.

Mediterranean Pasta Sauce

We just call it that; it was invented in Santa Cruz, California USA.

Open a couple of 8-ounce cans of tomato sauce and pour them into a large kettle. Add two pounds of ripe tomatoes that have been ground fine in your blender or food processor. Add $1/2$ cup each of virgin olive oil and red wine. Add oregano and chopped basil to taste. This is the subtle part that I learned from Ruth... don't overpower the tomatoes with herbs; just use enough to enhance their flavor.

Simmer for a couple of hours, add salt or soy sauce if desired. Pour over freshly boiled pasta and sprinkle the Parmesan.

Pick Poultry

Traditionally, chicken has been the meat of the poor. These days, with the high cost of beef, pork, and veal, it may well become the meat of the rich too. There are a thousand ways to fix chicken, but whichever way you choose, remember to save the bones and bits of skin to throw in your soup pot. Here we'll include just a few of our favorite recipes.

Out-West Chicken & Vegetables

2 chickens, cut into serving pieces
1 cup whole-wheat flour
1 teaspoon salt
$^1/_4$ teaspoon each marjoram, oregano, rosemary, and thyme
2 tablespoons oil
1 onion, sliced
$^1/_2$ pound mushrooms, sliced
$^1/_2$ green pepper, chopped
3 celery stalks, diced
2 cups stewed tomatoes
1 bay leaf

Wash and dry the chicken pieces, and shake them in a bag with flour, salt and herbs. Heat the oil in a heavy skillet, brown the chicken pieces in it, remove them and set aside.

To the drippings in the pan add the sliced onion and mushrooms, and sauté them until soft. Add the pepper, celery, stewed tomatoes, and bay leaf. Arrange the chicken pieces on top of the vegetables, cover the pan, and simmer gently until the chicken is tender. Serves 8.

Honey-Glazed Chicken

A 3-pound frying chicken, cut into serving pieces
salt and pepper
$1/4$ cup oil
$1/4$ cup honey
$1/4$ cup lemon juice
$1/4$ teaspoon paprika
$1/2$ teaspoon dry mustard

Wash and dry the chicken pieces, and season them with the salt and pepper. Heat the oil in the skillet and sauté the chicken, turning once to brown on both sides. Cover and cook over medium heat for 15 minutes. Blend the remaining ingredients and pour them over the chicken. Cook uncovered another 20 minutes, basting frequently. The chicken is done when a fork may be inserted easily. Serves 4-6.

This dish may also be baked in the oven. Arrange the chicken pieces, skin side down, in a shallow greased baking dish. Brush them with the marinade, cover the pan with foil, and bake 30 minutes at 350°. Remove the foil, turn the chicken, and brush it with the marinade. Increase the temperature to 400° and bake 15 to 20 minutes more, or until the chicken is golden brown and tender.

Island Chicken

A 3^1/$_2$ pound chicken, cut into serving pieces
^{1}/$_3$ cup soy sauce
2 tablespoons lemon juice
1 teaspoon sage
1 teaspoon salt
^{1}/$_2$ teaspoon pepper
1 teaspoon ginger
^{1}/$_2$ cup whole-wheat flour
^{1}/$_4$ cup oil
1 cup boiling water
1 large onion, cut in chunks

Place the washed chicken pieces in a bowl and pour over them the soy sauce, lemon juice, sage, salt, pepper, and ginger. Marinate for 1 hour or longer.

Lift the chicken pieces out and roll them in flour. Heat the oil in a skillet and fry the chicken until it's deep gold. Transfer it to a casserole or shallow pan, pour the boiling water in at the side, and arrange the onion chunks around. Pour the marinade over the chicken, cover, and bake at 350° for 1 hour. Serves 4-6.

HERBS, SAUCES & SALAD DRESSINGS

One of the real keys to staying happy on a low-cost diet is knowing how to use herbs, sauces, and salad dressings. Expensive foods like meats usually have plenty of flavor to begin with. But the less expensive staples like grains and beans often need something extra to give them character and interest. By adding just the right touch of flavoring ingredients, a smart cook can make plain fare taste every bit as good as steak and lobster.

Dressings and sauces for salads and main dishes can add important nutritional value to your meals, too.

Saving on Herbs

One good way to keep your budget at 99¢ a meal is to buy all your herbs in bulk. Most major cities have at least one wholesaler. Look in your yellow pages under herbs and spices.

Using your food co-op privileges, stock up on all the basics such as pepper, mustard, rosemary, thyme, sage, nutmeg, dill and so forth, buying as much as you can afford. Store in airtight containers, as most herbs lose their flavor within a year.

Herbs We Love

Well known to the ancients, herbs and seasonings have only recently begun to take their rightful place in modern American cooking. Salt and pepper, and a little cinnamon and nutmeg for baking, used to be just about the extent of the spice shelf in many a kitchen. But these days I often find myself tasting someone's new dish and wondering just how it got that intriguing flavor.

Recently I was trying to guess the special ingredient in a friend's salad dressing. When none of my guesses drew a nod, I finally had to give up. Turmeric, she told me. Turmeric! Who would have thought of it for salad dressing? It's a spice one usually associates with East Indian cooking. But as this experience illustrates, herbs and seasonings need not be typecast. Used with imagination, they often yield marvelous new taste sensations.

My all-time favorite herb is basil. A small potted basil plant purchased from your local nursery will grow fast, especially if you talk to it encouragingly. I simply love to pick the leaves and smell them and add them chopped up to omelets and salads and Italian dishes and anything else I can sneak them into. Once you have tried the following recipe, you may become a devoted basil fan, too.

Basil Pesto

1 cup fresh basil leaves, chopped
3 cloves garlic, peeled
$^1/_2$ cup freshly grated Parmesan or Romano Cheese
6 tablespoons olive oil
pinch of salt
$^1/_4$ cup finely chopped walnuts or pine nuts
$^1/_2$ cup chopped parsley
1 teaspoon dried marjoram, or a sprig of fresh marjoram

In Genoa you would use a mortar and pestle to make this sauce. A blender is a good substitute, however. Put in everything but the olive oil and blend, then add the oil a few drops at a time. Pour this sauce over about a pound of hot pasta (spaghetti, noodles, or macaroni) and toss. How do you say "yummy" in Italian? Serves 4-6.

Dill adds a subtle and intriguing flavor to many an otherwise flat-tasting dish. It can be easily grown at home or bought fresh in season at most vegetable markets. You can dry your own for use later in the winter, saving the seeds for flavoring as well.

Dill Bread

Breads flavored with herbs are heavenly, especially warm out of the oven. Try not to eat the whole loaf at once!

1 package yeast
$^1/_4$ cup lukewarm water
1 cup creamed cottage cheese
$^1/_4$ teaspoon baking soda
1 teaspoon salt
1 egg

1 tablespoon honey
1 tablespoon dried onion, or 2 tablespoons finely chopped raw
   onion
2 teaspoons dill seed
1 $^1/_4$ cups whole-wheat flour
1 $^1/_4$ cups unbleached white flour

Dissolve the yeast in the water. Gradually beat in the remaining ingredients. Let the dough rise in a covered bowl in a warm place until it doubles in bulk. Turn it onto a floured board and knead it until shiny. Let it rise again and form it into a loaf. Place it in a greased loaf pan and bake for 1 hour at 375°. Makes 1 loaf.

Sopa de Ajo (Garlic Soup)

Increased vitality, thicker hair, and a longer life are but a few of the many benefits credited to ordinary garlic — the "stinking onion," as Shakespeare called it. Known for centuries as a remedy for colds and other ills, it has now been found to be especially helpful to those suffering from high blood pressure. The major attraction of the ancient little vegetable, though, is still the special flavor it adds to the simplest dish.

You beat the seemingly high price of garlic, again, by growing your own. Then, sometime when you've gathered an overabundance, try this in celebration:

16-18 large cloves of garlic (that's right 16-18)
3 tablespoons oil or vegetable oil
2 quarts stock, preferably beef or chicken

Peel the garlic and sauté it in a large pot in the oil over very low heat, being careful not to let it burn. When it is soft, add the stock, and simmer for 20 minutes. Serves 6-8.

You can vary this soup by adding a variety of herbs such as thyme, rosemary, or bay leaves. To add more nutritional value and an interesting texture, stir in one or two beaten egg yolks just before serving. Noodles, rice, or potatoes might also be added for a more a filling soup.

Green Peas with Mint

Plant a rooted runner of mint in the shade near a faucet and it will spread everywhere. You can pick and dry the leaves and then crumble them for storage in jars. Steeped in boiling water, they make delicious and soothing tea. Chopped fresh mint is delicious on cooked carrots. Or try this with your freshly harvested peas:

1 tablespoon butter
1 pound peas, shelled
2 large lettuce leaves
1 teaspoon chopped fresh mint, or $^1/_2$ teaspoon crushed dried mint

Place the butter in the bottom of a saucepan, add the shelled peas, and put the lettuce leaves on top. Cook gently for about ten minutes or until the peas are just tender. Remove the lettuce leaves, add the mint, and stir gently. Serves 2.

Green Rice

Parsley is rich in potassium, one of the important minerals in our diet, and vitamins A and C. If eaten raw, it will sweeten your breath. Chopped in salads or used as a garnish, it adds color along with flavor. It's especially good in this recipe which can be served as a main dish.

Everyone should have fresh parsley in his herb garden because, like mint, it is so easy to grow. It can be used in hundreds of dishes. If you have a bumper crop, just put the surplus in plastic bags and freeze it, or dry it in the oven and store it in a jar.

1 cup milk
$^1/_4$ cup oil (olive or vegetable)
1 egg
1 clove garlic
1 cup diced cheddar cheese
1 cup parsley
1 cup cooked brown rice

Whirl the milk, oil, egg, and garlic in a blender. Gradually add the cheese and parsley. Blend well and pour over the rice. Mix together and bake in an oiled 1-quart casserole dish at 350° for 45 minutes. Serves 3-4.

Vinaigrette or How to Use Herbs to Make any Veggie Taste Good

Mix the following items: $^1/_2$ cup wine vinegar, olive oil, fresh lemon juice. Add your choice of herbs but be sure and include garlic or garlic powder, freshly ground pepper, a bit of cayenne, dry mustard, sea salt and fresh chopped chives. Let stand for several hours then add to cooked veggies for an overnight soak. This marinade can be used over again. An unusual variety evolves from the addition of a judicious amount of Balsamic vinegar, an Italian import that is expensive but lasts a long time because it is so flavorful.

Parsley Stuffed Peppers

In the summer when green peppers sometimes drop down in price, try this recipe:

6 large green peppers
1 cup boiling, salted water
1 clove garlic, minced
2 tablespoons chopped onion
4 tablespoons butter
1³/₄ cups bread crumbs
³/₄ teaspoon thyme
salt and pepper to taste
4 cups chopped fresh parsley

Cut off the tops of the peppers and remove the seeds and membrane. Place them in a pan with the boiling water and parboil for 5 minutes. Remove and drain.

Sauté the garlic and onion in the butter until tender. Add the bread crumbs and seasonings, and toss lightly. Blend in the parsley. Spoon the mixture into the peppers. Arrange them in an oiled casserole, cover, and bake 30 minutes at 375°. Remove the cover and bake 10 minutes longer. Serves 6.

Red Snapper With Rosemary

Rosemary is another herb one seems to encounter everywhere. Many people plant it as a border. If you can't find a friend who has some, it's also an easy herb to grow, adapting to most any soil and climate. Fresh or dried, it's wonderful with poultry, rabbit, lamb, or veal, and equally good with meat loaf or beans. Here it is adding character to a fish dish.

1 whole red snapper (1¹/₂-2 pounds)
1 teaspoon dried rosemary

salt and fresh ground pepper
6 tablespoons butter
2 tablespoons chopped lemon

The fish should be thoroughly cleaned and scaled. Dry the inside and sprinkle the cavity with the rosemary; then generously salt and pepper the outside.

Melt the butter in an ovenproof casserole and sauté the fish on one side for about 5 minutes, tilting the dish and spooning the hot butter over the fish. Turn it over and place it in a 425° oven for about 20 minutes, or until the fish flakes easily with a fork. Serve it with chopped lemon to garnish. Serves 6-8.

Pilaf

This term applies to almost any grain — rice, wheat, barley, couscous which is cooked in a special way and then served as a side dish like potatoes.

For this version you'll need 2 tablespoons butter, 1 cup long grain rice, a shake of salt and pepper plus about three cups of chicken broth or vegetable stock. Melt butter in large kettle and stir in rice and seasoning. Add broth and bring to simmer until rice is tender.

Next time try your homemade bulgar wheat instead of rice. You'll feel totally self-sufficient!

Sweet and Sour Red Cabbage

Always one of our top favorites, this side dish gets better as it ages. Also, it demonstrates how just one herb can transform a recipe, in this case, caraway seeds.

Chop a 2-pound head of red cabbage into thin slices. Core and peel two large green apples and chop fairly fine. Chop one large onion and 2 cloves of garlic. Place in large kettle and add 2 tablespoons of caraway seeds, 3 tablespoons sugar or honey,

$^1/_2$ teaspoon salt, dash of hot pepper sauce, 3 tablespoons vinegar and 3 tablespoons red wine.

Simmer slowly covered with a lid for 1 to 2 hours until tender and well-blended. Makes a fine accompaniment for any German-style dinner and is especially good cold.

Your Own Herb Teas

Many people who have discovered that caffeine and tannic acid are detrimental to their health are finding fragrant herb teas to be a pleasant and comforting substitute for the coffee and regular tea they used to find indispensable. Whether you live in the country or merely have the occasional opportunity to cross a vacant city lot, with a little luck you can gather suitable herbs for making your own herb teas at home.

Chamomile is a plant you're likely to encounter in many areas across the United States. Just nip off the flowers, dry them, and pour boiling water over a tablespoonful or two in the bottom of your teapot. Steep for a few minutes, and soon you'll have Peter Rabbit's favorite brew.

Mint is another ubiquitous plant, easily discovered in moist and shady spots if you aren't already growing some of your own. Pull off the leaves and dry them in the sun or in your oven; then crumble them into small bits and store them in an airtight container. Spearmint and peppermint are two common varieties of this plant, which can also be bought in a nursery.

Rosehips make a delicious tea and a mighty fine source of vitamin C. They are the little round seed pods found at the base of wild rose blooms. Harvest them in later summer when the petals are dropping off.

The leaves from blueberries, blackberries, and strawberries make a good addition to any combination of plants you may wish to dry for your tea. Blend them with dried flowers, such as hibiscus, orange blossoms, or passion flowers, and throw in some lemon grass, hawthorn berries, or rosemary. Some of the other popular ingredients in herb-tea blends include ginger, anise, dried orange or lemon peel, fennel, and clove. An especially nourishing addition would be dried alfalfa, which is nice combined with mint. Try experimenting with your own combination.

Herbs, published by Rodale Press, Emmaus, Pennsylvania, is a book that will help you recognize some of the plants we have been mentioning.

Some Reflections on This Book

It came about due to Ruth's emphatic rejection of a package of phony, plastic meat and our mutual agreement to point some new directions. One of the strongest motivations for this effort arrives when we see a hapless housewife, programmed with misinformation from TV sitcoms, listlessly pushing a grocery cart overloaded with colorful but expensive junk food.

Cultures are bonded by food. In China, for example, the standard greeting instead of "hello, how are you" is "have you eaten yet." Among people who would categorize themselves as "new age" we find a strong alliance created by cooking and serving dishes that are both tasty and healthy, conditions once thought to be contradictory.

What would happen in America if everyone opted for the 99¢ a meal lifestyle? Here are some speculations:

- We would save an enormous amount of money due to the virtual elimination of expensive packaging. At the present time, about 20% of the cost of everything in a supermarket is the container. Visualize plain brown bags with contents information printed thereon. This could be embellished with recipes.

- By eliminating the TV dinner genre, billions of kilowatts of power could be saved by shutting down expensive freezers. This cost is added to the general overhead of a market thus raising all prices.
- Elimination of what Nat Pritikin called "cosmetized garbage," the standard offering of most markets, would greatly improve America's overall health.
- If food is a human bond, then conversion to a natural diet would improve our complex interrelationships. By eating real food instead of processed disasters we would gain greater strength and comprehension. Picture the family that participates in grain-grinding, sprouting and cooperative meal preparation. Can you see the ancient tribal ties emerging?
- In summary, this presentation is intended to be more than a cookbook. It's intent is to provide some basic guidelines to a more natural life beginning with the key elements of good food and good health.

Super Sauces

How would spaghetti taste without sauce? And would French cuisine still be considered the ultimate without its béarnaise, bercy, and hollandaise? Of course not, for sauces like these can make the simplest dishes taste divine.

Now you're probably thinking already that fancy sauces are too expensive for the 99¢ a meal cook even to be reading about. But look at it this way. If you add 50¢ worth of hollandaise to 30¢ worth of steamed broccoli and celery, then for 80¢ you are going to have a regal dish for two. Similarly, it's the sauce that makes ordinary pasta, which is little more than wheat flour, into something exceptionally tasty and popular.

Obviously a sauce, even though costly, can make the difference between a dull dinner that no one wants to eat and one that brings kudos from all around the table. So here's an appealing selection of our favorite sauces.

Whole-Wheat Cream Sauce

2 tablespoons butter
2 tablespoons whole-wheat flour
1 cup milk
sea salt
paprika

Whirl all the ingredients in a blender; then pour them into a saucepan and heat, stirring constantly, until the sauce boils and thickens. With this method there will be no lumps to contend with. Makes 1 cup.

For a variation you can add grated onion, dill weed, fresh parsley, or grated cheese. Or you may want to add a bay leaf to the sauce while it's cooking and remove it just before serving.

Zesty Blue Cheese Sauce: Omit the paprika and add $^1/_4$ cup crumbled blue cheese and 1 teaspoon Worcestershire sauce.

Cheese and Anchovy Sauce: Omit the paprika and add $^1/_4$ pound grated cheese. Just before serving add 1 tablespoon chopped anchovy fillets.

Sauce for Vegetables

This rich and tasty sauce will make even the homeliest vegetables seem elegant. It will also add enough protein to qualify them as a main dish.

2 tablespoons butter or oil
2 tablespoons whole-wheat flour
$^1/_2$ teaspoon sea salt
$^1/_2$ teaspoon pepper
1 cup milk
1 cup grated cheddar cheese
$^1/_2$ teaspoon Worcestershire sauce
$^1/_2$ teaspoon paprika
pinch cayenne pepper
pinch dry mustard

Whirl all the ingredients in a blender; then pour them into a saucepan and heat, stirring constantly, until the sauce boils and thickens. Pour it over cooked cauliflower, broccoli, asparagus, celery, peas, string beans, Brussels sprouts, Swiss chard, cabbage, or potatoes, or any combination of these vegetables. Makes 2 cups.

Lemon-Mushroom Sauce

$1/4$ cup butter
2 tablespoons chopped onions
$1/4$ cup sliced mushrooms
1 tablespoon lemon juice
$1/2$ teaspoon thyme
$1/2$ teaspoon sea salt
1 teaspoon cornstarch
$1/4$ cup water

Melt the butter in a saucepan and add the onion and mushrooms. Cook gently for about 5 minutes. Stir in the lemon juice, thyme, and salt. Mix the cornstarch with water and add it to the saucepan, stirring until the sauce thickens. Makes 1 cup.

Red and Green Tartar Sauce

1 cup mayonnaise
$1/2$ cup yogurt
2 tablespoons minced onion
$1/2$ green pepper, minced
$1/2$ red pepper, minced
1 teaspoon lemon juice
1 tablespoon finely chopped dill pickle
2 tablespoons minced parsley
$1/2$ teaspoon each salt and pepper

Combine all of these ingredients in a bowl and beat them until well blended. Chill. Makes 2 cups.

Looking Pretty

While we're on the subject of making dishes taste more appetizing with herbs, sauces, and so on, let's stop to talk for a minute about making them look more enticing on the plate. A single sprig of fresh green parsley will pick up a dish of lima beans and ham hocks at least 100 percent! A radish or two deftly carved into roses will spark the plainest salad. Just the merest dash of paprika will render a plain fried egg or cheese dish colorful and inviting. And so it goes — little inexpensive garnishes can make all the difference to plain-looking meals.

Here are some more tips for making a 50¢ supper look like a $10 banquet:

- A few chopped nuts can transform a plain pudding, vegetable, or sauce into a stellar dish.
- Leave the peel on your red apples the next time you make a fruit salad.
- Always try to sprinkle some bread crumbs, cheese, or cracker crumbs over your casseroles to give them that appetizing crispy brown topping.
- Make a point of serving vegetables of contrasting colors — carrots, yellow squash, or sweet potatoes with green beans, spinach, or zucchini. Pale vegetables like cauliflower, celery, onions, and potatoes particularly need a color accent.
- A plain pudding seems twice as delicious with just a few red berries on top.
- Try the julienne approach: cut cheese, cooked meats, or vegetables into matchstick strips, and add them to salads, Chinese dishes, or whatever.

Aioli

Even a tablespoonful of a sauce like Aioli can bring about a wonderful transformation. Try it as a dip for raw vegetables and as an accompaniment to cold meats, fish, or hard-boiled eggs.

3 cloves garlic
sea salt
2 egg yolks or 1 whole egg, beaten
$^1/_2$ cup olive oil and $^1/_2$ cup safflower oil
juice of 1 lemon
1 teaspoon water

Peel the garlic and mince it or pound it in a mortar (if you don't own a mortar, you may crush the garlic on a wooden chopping block). Add the garlic and salt to the egg yolks. Then, beating constantly, slowly add the oil, drop by drop. After using about half the oil, you can increase the flow. Add the lemon juice and water at the end. We have also made this in a blender or mixer, but the texture is best when the sauce is beaten by hand with a wire whisk. Makes $1^1/_2$ cups.

Dressing Up Your Salads

As the old saying goes, "It takes five people to make a good salad: a spendthrift for oil, a miser for vinegar, a counselor for salt, a madman for mixing, and a genius for herbs."

What sauce is to pasta, dressing is to a bowl of salad greens. Eating these raw vegetables plain is not a bad experience; however, when you dribble over them a few tablespoons of French dressing with some crumbled Roquefort, you have a true gourmet's treat. As with sauces, money spent on dressings is coin well applied. After all, if you can lend excitement to a 25¢ bowl of raw vegetables with another 25¢ worth of some exotic dressing, you'll have a pleasing and healthful course for two at just 50¢.

Here are selections from the thousands of dressings to be found around the world.

French Herb Dressing

You could pour this over the most humble weeds you picked in your nearest vacant lot and think you were dining in an elegant restaurant.

3 cups oil
1 cup vinegar

juice of 1 lemon
2 teaspoons sea salt
freshly ground pepper
4 cloves garlic
$^1/_2$ cup parsley
$^1/_2$ green pepper, chopped
2 large green onions, chopped
1 teaspoon mustard seed
$^1/_2$ teaspoon each dill seed, marjoram, basil
$^1/_2$ cup water

Combine the oil, vinegar, lemon juice, salt and pepper in a large container. Blend the remaining ingredients together and add them to the first mixture. Makes 5 cups.

Ruth's French Dressing

$1^1/_2$ cups safflower oil
$^3/_4$ cup cider vinegar
1 teaspoon salt
$^1/_2$ teaspoon freshly ground pepper
1 tablespoon ketchup
1 clove garlic

Pour the ingredients into a jar, shake it well, and let the clove of garlic soak for at least a day ahead of use. This dressing will keep several days. Makes $2^1/_3$ cups.

Roquefort Dressing: to 1 cup of Ruth's French Dressing add 2 ounces of crumbled Roquefort cheese (or blue cheese, whichever is least expensive). Shake well.

Lemon Dressing

$^2/_3$ cup oil
$^1/_3$ cup lemon juice
1 clove garlic, minced
$^1/_2$ teaspoon prepared mustard
sea salt and freshly ground pepper

Blend all ingredients and chill. For a nice variation on this, add a bit of honey and 2 or 3 teaspoons of toasted sesame seeds. Makes 1 cup.

Yogurt Dressing

Delicious over cold seafood, sliced tomatoes, cole slaw, green salad, or any cooked, chilled vegetable.

4 tablespoons lemon juice
$^1/_4$ cup oil
$^1/_2$ cup water
2 tablespoons honey
4 tablespoons grated onion
2 teaspoons dill weed
1 teaspoon celery seed
2 teaspoons sea salt
$^1/_4$ cup chopped parsley
pinch cayenne
1 cup homemade yogurt
1 cup mayonnaise

Mix all ingredients in the blender except the yogurt and mayonnaise. Fold these in gently at the end in order to preserve their custard-like consistency. Makes $3^1/_3$ cups.

Green Dressing

Sometimes you can find watercress growing wild in a small brook or stream, if you're lucky enough to have a clean one nearby. Bring some home to put in your salad, and be sure to reserve enough for this zesty dressing.

1 cup mayonnaise
$^1/_2$ cup homemade yogurt
2 green onions, sliced, tops and all
$^1/_2$ cup minced watercress
$^1/_2$ cup chopped parsley
1 clove garlic, minced
1 tablespoon tarragon vinegar
sea salt
freshly ground pepper

Whirl these ingredients in the blender for a smooth green dressing. Makes $2^1/_2$ cups.

Thousand Island Yogurt Dressing

1 cup mayonnaise
$^1/_2$ cup yogurt
$^1/_2$ cup ketchup

Blend and serve on any kind of lettuce. Makes 2 cups.

Creamy Fresh Herb Dressing

$^2/_3$ cup mayonnaise
$^2/_3$ cup homemade yogurt
2 tablespoons chopped parsley and chives
1 teaspoon each chopped fresh tarragon, thyme, and basil
sea salt, paprika, freshly ground pepper

Combine all the ingredients in a bowl and refrigerate for several hours until thoroughly blended. You may substitute other fresh herbs, such as marjoram, sage, or mint, according to what you have available. Makes $1^1/2$ cups.

Be Prepared

The motto of the Boy Scouts seems particularly appropriate in this era of continuous future shock. Relax, rest easy with a supply of 99¢ a meal comestibles... here's our current larder.

- Lots of pasta; noodles, spaghetti, lasagna.
- Plenty of grains such as wheat, rye, corn, and oats, ground and unground. We have a hand-mill as well as two blenders and our beloved Oskar. Our trailer generator would run these in case power failed.
- Enough tomatoes in cans to last for quite a spell.
- Dried fruits including dates, raisins, apples.
- A small amount of canned items such as tuna, beans, chilis.
- Lots of dried beans in several varieties.
- Plenty of herbs and enough bay trees nearby to supply the entire U.S. indefinitely.
- Sea salt , pepper, dry chilis.
- Soy milk in paper cartons.
- Frozen fruits like blueberries and pineapple. Not much frozen, because a power outage would cause a rapid meltdown and our generator does not have sufficient wattage to handle the refrigerator.
- Rice, potatoes, onions, garlic and similar fast turnover items.
- Plenty of water in glass gallons.
- Alternative ways to cook.

We think that the above food bank would see us through almost any geological, social or miscellaneous cataclysm. And if it didn't we are pretty adept at wildfoods, scrounging, fishing and gardening. So if you would like to feel comfort-able, we suggest laying in your favorite storables. With 50 pound sacks of corn selling for about $15 it wouldn't cost too much to have a substantial supply of 99¢ a meal staples around the house.

All the luscious fruits have a special place in the 99¢ a meal diet. This huge class of fresh foods has lots of vitamins and minerals; they're a good source of food fiber; and they're low in fats. Gorillas, after all, who are ten times stronger than humans, live on a diet of fresh fruits and nuts alone! But we can get the same nutritional benefits and maybe more from vegetables. So you might say that the special value of the fruit family is not nutritional but esthetic — pure eating pleasure. No other kind of food can top fruit for beautiful color, texture, and aroma. And how about flavor?

This chapter is really devoted to treats that are healthy, delicious, and cheap. Along with some of our favorite fruit recipes, mainly for breakfast and dessert, we've added a section on using two other great natural sweeteners — honey and carob. You can eat well on 99¢ a meal, and that means indulging in an occasional sweet treat too!

Apples, Apricots, Bananas...

Now the first step to enjoying fruit on 99¢ a meal is getting it fresh, ripe and natural at a low, low cost. As usual, the supermarket is the worst bet, even though prices may drop dramatically at the height of the season. What are your alternatives?

If you've got some yard space available, how about growing some dwarf fruit trees?

Look around your neighborhood; you might find a volunteer fruit tree or two growing on an abandoned piece of property. Last year we harvested several boxes of apples and figs from trees that apparently belonged to no one.

Local growers will often let you pick your own at a big discount. Even better, sometimes you can pick your own for free. Once, while driving from Stockton, California, to a village in the Sierra foothills, I passed a cherry orchard alive with pickers. I stopped to watch and discovered that all the cherries that had fallen to the ground were free to anyone who wanted them. Apparently the law says that if they touch the ground, they can't go to market. So I promptly got out my trusty burlap bag (I always keep one in the trunk of my car) and proceeded to pick 5 or 6 pounds of the ripest, sweetest cherries I've ever eaten. All they needed was a quick rinse and they were ready for the fruit bowl, cherry cobbler, or preserves.

Always keep an eye peeled for good bargains at roadside stands. Then eat a lot, dry a lot, and can what you can.

The best recipe for fruits is to simply eat them fresh as soon as they're ripe, without any cooking, coating, processing, or fumbling by the corporate state. But it's fun to play around with them too and here are some good ways to do it.

Apple Flannel Cakes

2 eggs
$1^1/2$ cups sour milk
2 tablespoons melted butter, margarine, or oil
1 cup whole-wheat pastry flour
2 tablespoons date sugar
1 teaspoon vanilla
$^1/2$ teaspoon cinnamon
$^1/4$ teaspoon soda
2 apples, peeled, cored, and quartered

Put all the ingredients in a blender and whirl for 1 minute. Heat a griddle until fairly hot, pour on the batter, and tilt the griddle from side to side to spread the batter out thinner. Continue cooking as you would any pancake.

These may be served with honey, maple syrup, or black-strap molasses. But try them plain first, and you may decide they don't need any embellishment at all. That's how we feel about them. Makes 6 to 8 pancakes.

Johnny Appleseed's Special

This delectable dessert requires no cooking at all.

4 apples
1 tablespoon honey
1 tablespoon lemon juice

$^1/_2$ cup chopped dates
1 cup homemade yogurt
4 tablespoons chopped almonds or other nuts

Core the apples and shred them, skins and all, into a large bowl. Sprinkle them with the honey, lemon juice, and dates. Add a dollop of yogurt, and top them with the nuts for garnish. Serves 4.

Apple Whip

2 cups applesauce
2 envelopes plain gelatin
2 tablespoons honey
2 teaspoons lemon juice
2 egg whites
nutmeg and cinnamon

Place 1 cup of the applesauce in a double boiler over boiling water. Add the gelatin, stir, and let it dissolve. Remove it from the heat and add the honey, lemon juice, and remaining cup of applesauce.

Let it cool, and refrigerate until it's almost set. Beat the egg whites until they're stiff and fold them into the apple mixture. Return it to the refrigerator until set. Scoop into serving glasses and top with nutmeg and cinnamon. Mmmmm. Serves 4-6.

Apple Crisp

A worldwide favorite that appears in the culinary records of many cultures. Try it this way.

8 large apples
$^1/_4$ cup honey
2 tablespoons lemon juice
$^1/_2$ teaspoon cinnamon

$^{1}/_{2}$ cup rolled oats
$^{1}/_{2}$ cup wheat germ
$^{1}/_{3}$ cup fresh bran
$^{1}/_{4}$ cup brown rice flour
$^{1}/_{4}$ cup ground dried dates
$^{1}/_{4}$ cup safflower oil or melted butter

Wash, core and slice 8 large apples. Mix the honey, lemon juice, and cinnamon, and add them to the apples. Toss to mix and coat. Place the mixture in a buttered baking dish and add a topping made of the remaining ingredients, mixed well and sprinkled over the apples to cover.

Bake in a preheated oven at about 325° for 35 to 45 minutes, or until the apples are tender. Remove and see how much cooling time you can allow before it's totally devoured by apple bandits. Serves 6 normal people, or 2 apple bandits!

Wild Bill's Favorite Apple Pie

Good old apple pie. If you're going to economize on food, you need to have some rewards, and this is it. No sense in making just one, so this recipe makes two large pies.

4 cups freshly ground whole-wheat flour
1 teaspoon sea salt
$1^{1}/_{4}$ cups oil (sesame, soy, safflower)
ice water
8 cups peeled and sliced organic cooking apples
2 tablespoons honey
2 teaspoons cinnamon
2 tablespoons arrowroot
lemon or orange juice
sesame seeds (optional)

Mix the flour, salt, and oil. Add enough ice water to make a stiff dough; roll it out and drape it over 2 pie tins, saving the balance for the top.

Place the apples on the pie crusts, almost filling the tins. Then mix and add the honey, cinnamon, arrowroot, and a squeeze or two of lemon or orange juice. Top with the remaining pie crusts, prick the tops with a fork, and flute the edges. Brush the tops with melted butter.

I like to sprinkle sesame seeds on top, since they brown nicely and taste great. Bake at about 350° for about 45 minutes, or until the crusts are a rich golden brown.

Lamb's Wool

This is an old pioneer treat that will taste just as good in 1997 as it did in 1777.

8 large cored apples
2 quarts apple cider
$^1/_2$ cup honey
2 tablespoons mixed pickling spices
cinnamon sticks

Bake the apples in your oven until they're very soft. Whirl them in a blender or otherwise reduce them to pulp. Next combine the apple cider with the honey and pickling spices. Stir until the honey dissolves. Strain out the spices. Combine the pulp and the hot cider mixture, heat, and serve in mugs. Provide cinnamon stick stirring rods; you may need long-handled spoons if the drink is too thick. Serves 8-10.

Applesauce Pudding

This recipe will use up all your leftover crumbs.

2 cups crumbs (cookie or bread)
2 tablespoons honey

1 teaspoon cinnamon
2 tablespoons wheat germ
4 tablespoons sesame seeds
4 tablespoons chopped almonds
1 tablespoon vegetable oil (optional)
6 cups applesauce

Combine the crumbs, honey, cinnamon, wheat germ, sesame seeds, and almonds. Add a bit of cold-press oil if the mixture is too dry. Layer the crumb mixture alternately with the applesauce in a buttered casserole, and bake for 20 minutes in a 300° oven until heated through. Serves 6.

Goes Well With Apple Pudding

Slice apples into bottom of baking dish. Sprinkle $1/4$ cup sugar and $1/2$ teaspoon cinnamon over apples and add 2 tablespoons butter and $1/4$ cup hot water. Beat one egg and add $1/2$ cup honey. Sift $1/3$ cup whole wheat flour, 1 teaspoon baking powder and pinch of salt. Spread batter on top of apples. Bake 30 minutes at 375° for 10 minutes, then at 350° until done.

Apricot-Walnut Muffins

Grind your flour from fresh whole-grain wheat, gather some windfalls in a local walnut orchard, and of course, get your apricots right from the tree. But even if you have to buy some of your ingredients in the store, you can still make these on a 99¢ a meal budget.

$1 1/2$ cups finely ground whole-wheat flour
2 teaspoons baking power
$1/2$ teaspoon salt
$1/2$ teaspoon cinnamon
$1/3$ cup honey
$1/2$ cup finely chopped home-dried apricots

$^1/_2$ cup chopped walnuts
1 egg, slightly beaten
1 cup milk
$^1/_4$ cup salad oil

Mix all ingredients, stirring just until blended. Spoon the batter in muffin tins and bake at 425° for 20 to 25 minutes. Makes about 2 dozen.

Apricot Oatmeal

There's a tasty symbiosis between oatmeal and apricots.

4 cups water
2 cups rolled oats
$^1/_4$ teaspoon salt
$^1/_2$ cup finely cut home-dried apricots
1 teaspoon cinnamon
$^1/_2$ cup wheat germ
milk and honey (optional)

Bring the water to a boil and gradually add the oatmeal and dried apricots. Simmer, stirring occasionally, for 5 minutes. Remove from the heat and stir in the cinnamon and wheat germ. Serve with milk and honey if desired. Serves 6.

Dry Your Own

If you live anywhere near where apricots are grown and have the opportunity to pick your own as Ruth and I did in the summertime, go for it! But barring that opportunity, if you buy them by the lug box when they are at the height of the season, the price should remain low enough for you to afford this marvelous fruit on your 99¢ a meal budget. Then you can do as we do, and dry all those you don't expect to be able to eat right away.

Lay them between screens or on one screen with a coarsely woven cloth on top to keep off the flies, and leave them in the sun for two or three days. Turn them occasionally while drying. An alternative method is to dry them in the oven set at its lowest temperature with the door propped slightly open. Leave them in all night.

When completely dry, store these treasures in tightly capped jars for use all the rest of the year. When you price dried apricots in the store, you'll feel mightily smug.

Apricot Cream

This may be made with peaches, berries or prunes as well.

1 tablespoon unflavored gelatin
$^1/_4$ cup cold water
2 cups apricot puree made by blending $1^1/_2$ cups fresh apricots with $^1/_2$ cup water
1 egg, separated
4 tablespoons honey
1 teaspoon lemon juice
$^3/_4$ cup homemade yogurt

Dissolve the gelatin in the cold water. Blend the apricot puree with the egg yolk, honey, and lemon juice, and heat it in a saucepan until it just begins to boil. Remove it from the heat and stir in the softened gelatin. Chill until it begins to set.

Fold in the yogurt and then the stiffly beaten egg white. Chill again, in an oiled mold if desired, and serve. Serves 6.

Avocado Sherbet

1 large or 2 small ripe avocados
juice and rind of 1 lemon
4 tablespoons honey

1 cup milk
$^1/_2$ cup milk powder
pinch sea salt

Remove the skin and seed from the avocado and place it in a blender together with the remaining ingredients. Whirl until smooth. Pour the mixture into an ice tray and freeze it until firm, stirring once or twice. This can be served garnished with fresh citrus. Serves 4.

Play It Safe — Buy Bananas

Often, when I'm traveling along in my GMC camper, I make a stop in a small town to see what horrors are being sold in the local market. I'm seldom disappointed: row on row of packaged catastrophes plus that great phosphoric acid and sugar combination, the Pause that Refreshes! But — and it's a big but — one can almost always spot some bananas. There's not too much the food industry can do to a banana, though it's rumored that some are artificially ripened with strange gases. Nonetheless, bananas offer reasonably good nutritional value and a low incidence of chemical intervention.

And the price is right, too — at this writing only about 35¢ a pound. If you come across a super banana bargain, don't hesitate to stock up. You can peel and dry those you can't immediately eat in a 200° oven with the door slightly open. My grandson thinks they're better than candy.

Do remember that bananas should not be eaten until every bit of green has disappeared; otherwise they're difficult to digest.

Broiled or Fried Bananas

Peel 1 banana per person. Cut them in half lengthwise and place them flat side down in a shallow baking dish or pan.

Broil for 3 minutes, not too close to the flame. Turn them over and drizzle honey over each piece. Sprinkle shredded coconut over the honey and broil another 3 minutes, being careful not to let them burn.

Bananas may also be fried in butter and served with a squirt of lemon juice for a simple yet fantastic-tasting dessert.

Banana Bread

2 mashed bananas
$^1/_2$ cup honey
2 eggs
$^1/_2$ cup buttermilk or sour milk
2 tablespoons safflower oil
2 teaspoons vanilla
2 cups whole-wheat flour
$^1/_2$ teaspoon baking soda
$^1/_4$ teaspoon ground cloves
$^1/_2$ cup chopped walnuts

Mash the bananas with a fork or in a blender; add the honey, eggs, buttermilk, oil, and vanilla. Blend the flour, soda and cloves, and add them to the liquid mixture. Fold in the walnuts and pour the batter into an oiled loaf pan. Bake at 350° for 50 minutes to 1 hour. Makes 1 loaf.

Huevos con Platano (Eggs with Bananas)

Bananas prepared in this Mexican way are usually served as a vegetable. They're delicious with fried chicken. If you prefer them as a dessert, cook them in part butter and part oil and make a honey or fruit-syrup topping.

3 bananas
juice of 1 lemon

2 eggs
$^1/_4$ cup whole-wheat pastry flour
milk
2 tablespoons vegetable oil

Peel and split the bananas lengthwise, and cut each piece in half. Dip them in lemon juice. Make a batter of the eggs, flour, and a little milk, thoroughly blended. Dip the banana slices in the batter and fry them in the oil over medium heat until brown, turning when partly cooked. Serves 6.

Banana Shake

This is a good way to begin taking brewer's yeast, which is a wonderful source of all the B vitamins. You can increase the amount of yeast as you get used to the taste.

1 banana
2 heaping tablespoons milk powder
2 cups cold water
1 tablespoon brewer's yeast
1 tablespoon blackstrap molasses
1 tablespoon honey
1 tablespoon lecithin

Whirl all the ingredients in a blender until creamy. Serves 2.

Frontier Blackberry Cobbler

Of course, you can make this with other kinds of berries and fruit as well.

$1^1/_2$ cups whole wheat pastry flour
2 teaspoons baking powder
$1^1/_2$ cups milk

$^3/_4$ cup honey
$^1/_2$ cup melted butter
2 cups blackberries
$^1/_4$ teaspoon cinnamon

Mix the flour and baking powder, and add the milk, honey, and butter. Place the berries in a buttered casserole and sprinkle the cinnamon over them. Pour the batter on top and bake for 45 minutes at 350°. This is extra good served warm with a little cream or even milk poured over it. Serves 6.

Berries for Free

Berries grow wild in many places throughout the U.S. We've found tons going completely to waste in parts of Oregon and California. I recall some of the biggest berries I've ever seen growing on the shores of Mercer Island in Lake Washington near Seattle. They were easily the size of a big man's thumb. And there were few takers for this luscious delicacy!

Check around your neighborhood. Often clumps of wild blackberry bushes are concealed by willow and tule thickets. It's likely you'll find berries growing near bodies of water, since they love to have a bountiful supply. Once you locate some, dive in with both hands, being wary of the thorns, of course.

Besides eating them fresh, you may preserve them by canning, whirl them in your blender drinks, or put them on top of homemade corn cakes for the breakfast treat of your life. Or try another old-time favorite, blackberry cobbler.

Baked Pears

6 firm pears
$^1/_2$ cup honey

$^1/_2$ cup water
1 teaspoon ground ginger
2 tablespoons lemon juice

Cut the pears in half and core them. Arrange them in a baking dish. Combine the remaining ingredients, boil for 5 minutes, and pour over the pears. Cover and bake at 350° for 15 minutes, or until just tender. Uncover and place under a broiler for a few minutes until glazed. Serves 6.

Creamy Prune Bread Pudding

$^3/_4$ cup pitted prunes, cut up
1 cup whole-wheat bread cubes
1 cup scalded milk
$^1/_4$ cup butter
$^1/_4$ cup honey or date sugar
1 cup homemade yogurt
3 eggs
1 tablespoon lemon juice
nutmeg

Put the prunes and bread cubes in a bowl and pour the scalded milk over them. Set aside. Cream the butter and honey, and add the yogurt. Beat in the eggs one at a time. Add the lemon juice and the bread mixture. Turn into a buttered casserole or baking pan and sprinkle nutmeg on top.

Bake in a pan of hot water at 350° for 45 minutes or until a knife blade comes out clean. May be served warm or cold. Serves 6.

Fruit Snow

1 cup chopped fresh fruit
2 egg whites
1 teaspoon honey

Puree the fruit in the blender and then heat it in a saucepan to the boiling point. Remove from the heat and cool. Beat the egg whites until stiff, gradually adding the honey, and fold them into the fruit puree. Pile into glasses or small sauce dishes, and chill before serving. Serves 2.

Yogurt-Fruit Sherbet

2 cups homemade yogurt
2 cups chopped fresh fruit

Pour the yogurt into refrigerator trays and freeze it until it's almost firm. Remove it to a bowl and beat it. Fold in the fruit (which may be sweetened with honey) and return the mixture to the trays. Freeze it again until almost firm, beat it again, and return it to the freezer until ready to serve. Serves 6.

Variety is the Spice of Life

When the first edition of this book was written the average produce stand had less than 100 items and most were quite basic. Today the larger veggie and fruit purveyors boast more than 400 different items. They include out-of-season grapes, all kinds of tropical fruits, unusual vegetables such as tomatillo and radichio plus variations of standard items; who ever heard of a Fuji apple or kiwi ten years ago?

This revolution in food merchandising is a great plus for everyone. For the 99¢ a meal people there is a special boon. As those expensive papayas and mangos approach their over-ripe state, start making offers. If you get to know your produce person, you will get lots of bargains.

Divine Dates & Raisins

A favorite in Egypt since ancient times, dates have been found in the tombs of the pharaohs still edible. Actually, their immortality is due to a high natural sugar content — about 70 percent — so go easy. But nothing beats dates when you decide to indulge in a treat, and you can always tell yourself that they're rich in minerals, too.

When bought by the lug box through a natural-food store or co-op, dates can cost as low as $1.88 a pound. They provide an ideal natural sweetener for cooked cereals. Chopped and cooked up in a little water, they can be spooned over homemade ice cream or custard, or whirled in the blender with milk to make a date shake.

An old timer and still a favorite in our family around Christmas time is stuffed dates. Pit as many as you wish, stuff them with cream cheese and press half a walnut into each. Prettily arranged and wrapped, they make a welcome gift.

Like dates, raisins are great for adding a bit of natural sweetness to breads, cereals, cookies, and puddings, while supplying some important nutrients like iron, potassium, magnesium, and calcium. Their uses range from a simple treat in your child's lunchbox all the way up to a garnish for an exotic curry. Raisins are a must in backpack mix: combine them with peanuts and sunflower seeds, or whatever nuts, seeds, or other dried fruits strike your fancy, and take them along for great munching on your next hike.

Apple-Date Slaw

2 large apples, chopped
1 cup chopped dates
$^1/_2$ head cabbage, finely sliced
2 tablespoons honey
$^1/_4$ cup mayonnaise
2 tablespoons yogurt
juice of half a lemon
sea salt to taste

Place the apples, dates, and cabbage in a bowl. Make a dressing by mixing the remaining ingredients. Pour the dressing over the salad and toss well. Serves 6.

Grey Bears

Every week we receive a large brown bag full of veggies, fruits, bread and other edibles. It is presented by the Grey Bears, an organization of seniors dedicated to helping others. To begin, they solicited food from farmers and ranchers gleaning the fields and orchards after regular harvests. They also asked bakeries and dairies for their surplus items. In time they built a firm base of donated foods that arrive at the GB warehouse all year. Senior volunteers sort, package and deliver to those who request the otherwise wasted foods. For more information on this worthy plan of action, write the authors in care of the publisher.

Oatmeal-Date Muffins

2 cups rolled oats
1¹/₂ cups sour milk or buttermilk
2 tablespoons honey
1 egg
2 tablespoons oil
1 cup whole- wheat flour
1 teaspoon baking soda
1 teaspoon sea salt
¹/₂ cup chopped dates

Add the oats to the sour milk or buttermilk and let them stand an hour or so. Beat in the honey, egg, and oil. Blend the flour, baking soda, and salt, and add them all at once, stirring only until the flour disappears. Fold the dates in last.

Bake in greased muffin pans for 30 to 35 minutes in a 400° oven. Makes about 2 dozen.

Date-Rice Pudding

2 cups chopped dates
1 ¹/₂ cups raw brown rice
2¹/₂ cups milk made from powder
¹/₂ cup honey
1 egg, beaten
1 teaspoon cinnamon
¹/₂ teaspoon nutmeg
¹/₄ teaspoon ground ginger
1 cup homemade yogurt

Cook the dates in water to cover until soft; drain. Cook the rice in the milk until tender. Stir in the honey, egg, and spices. Spread half of the rice into an oiled 1-quart casserole. Cover it with half of the cooked dates. Repeat the two layers.

Bake at 350° for 25 minutes. Remove and cook. Spread the yogurt over the top and chill before serving. Serves 6-8.

Date-Coconut Chews

1 cup water mixed with $^1/_2$ cup milk powder
1 cup dates, pitted and chopped
1 cup shredded coconut
$^1/_2$ cup chopped walnuts
$^1/_2$ cup whole-wheat flour
2 teaspoons vanilla
$^1/_8$ teaspoon sea salt

Mix all the ingredients thoroughly with a fork. Then form the dough into small balls, place them on an oiled cookie sheet, and bake them at 325° for 12 minutes or until lightly browned. Makes 18-20 chews.

Some years ago we bought an entire lug box of beautiful fresh dates for just $6, or less than 30¢ a pound. There was a catch to the deal. The dates had been nibbled on by birds while they were on the tree. But my reasoning was this: the birds, free to sample any date, would choose the sweetest ones! And here's what we made with some of this big bargain.

Date Streusel Coffee Cake

$^1/_2$ cup date sugar
$^1/_3$ cup finely ground whole-wheat flour
2 teaspoons cinnamon
$^3/_4$ cup chopped walnuts
$^1/_3$ cup butter
$^1/_3$ cup honey
2 eggs
$1^1/_2$ cups finely ground whole-wheat flour

1 teaspoon baking powder
$^1/_2$ teaspoon baking soda
$^1/_2$ teaspoon sea salt
$^1/_2$ teaspoon nutmeg
$^2/_3$ cup yogurt

Mix the sugar, $^1/_3$ cup of flour, cinnamon, and walnuts, and set them aside. Blend the butter, honey, and eggs; add $1^1/_2$ cups flour and the baking powder, soda, salt and nutmeg. Stir in the yogurt. Pour half of the batter into a square baking pan and top it with half of the walnut mixture; then repeat the layers.

Bake at 350° for 25 to 30 minutes. Serves 8.

Oatmeal-Raisin Rolls

Feature these as a main breakfast item with a glass of milk or a little cottage cheese and a pot of fragrant herb tea.

1 package active dry yeast
3 tablespoons lukewarm water
$^1/_2$ cup rolled oats
2 tablespoons cooking oil
$^1/_2$ cup honey
1 teaspoon salt
1 cup boiling water
$^3/_4$ cup coarsely chopped raisins
$2^1/_2$ cups whole-wheat flour
melted butter

Sprinkle the yeast into the lukewarm water, and stir until it is dissolved. Combine the oats, oil, honey, salt, and boiling water; let the mixture cool to lukewarm, and add the raisins, yeast, and flour. Mix to a moderately stiff dough. Turn it out onto a floured board and knead lightly a few minutes.

Return it to the bowl, cover, and let it rise for 45 to 60 minutes, or until it doubles in size. Form the dough into smooth balls about $1^1/2$ inches in diameter. Place the rolls about $^1/2$ inch apart in a greased pan. Cover and let them rise 35 to 40 minutes until doubled. Brush the tops with melted butter.

Bake in a 375° oven 20 to 25 minutes, or until nicely browned. Makes about 18 rolls.

Boston Brown Bread

A New England favorite for over two centuries. Traditionally this bread was steamed, but we like it just baked like any other.

1 cup raisins
$^3/4$ cup corn meal
$^3/4$ cup whole-wheat or graham flour
$1^1/2$ cups sifted unbleached flour
$1^1/2$ teaspoons salt
$1^1/2$ teaspoons baking soda
1 teaspoon baking powder
1 egg, beaten
1 cup buttermilk
$^3/4$ cups molasses
2 tablespoons vegetable oil

Combine the raisins, corn meal, and whole-wheat flour. Sift the unbleached flour with the salt, soda, and baking powder. Stir in the raisin mixture. Combine the eggs, buttermilk, molasses, and oil, and add them to the dry mixture, stirring just until moistened. Spoon the batter into a greased 10x5x3-inch loaf pan.

Bake at 350° for 50 minutes, or until a toothpick comes out clean when inserted in the center. Let the bread cool in the pan for 10 minutes before removing. Makes 1 loaf.

Carrot-Raisin Muffins

1 egg
$^1/_2$ cup milk
$^1/_4$ cup oil
$^1/_3$ cup honey
1 cup grated raw carrot
$1^1/_2$ cups finely ground whole-wheat flour
2 tablespoons baking powder
$^1/_2$ teaspoon salt
$^1/_2$ teaspoon cinnamon
$^1/_2$ cup raisins

Whirl the egg, milk, oil, honey, and carrot in a blender. Pour the mixture into a bowl and gently stir in the remaining ingredients. Pour into greased muffin tins and bake at 350° for 25 minutes. Makes about 2 dozen.

Revisions Invited

We plan to revise this book as long as we can. So please send your comments and suggestions to us at Holy Terra, PO Box 832, Soquel, CA 95073. We'll also be happy to answer any questions you might have. Thanks for tuning in. Ruth and Bill Kaysing.

Honey and Carob

Everyone has a hankering for something sweet now and then. Fortunately, there are many ways to satisfy that sweet tooth without resorting to refined white sugar, which is nutritionally worthless and even damaging to your health. One alternative, of course, is honey, a natural sugar which contains healthful minerals and vitamins. Others are date sugar, molasses, and maple syrup. And there's a wide variety of dried fruits that can be eaten by themselves or added to various desserts.

Honey is the most logical substitute for sugar in most recipes, but bear in mind that because of its sweetness you won't need to use as much. If a recipe calls for $^3/_4$ cup sugar, substitute $^1/_2$ cup honey. Since any kind of sugar is harmful if used to excess, we hesitate to recommend even honey too strongly. It's a fine condiment, but use it sparingly. Honey keeps extremely well. If you are setting some foods by for later use, include a gallon or two of honey. While it may crystallize, it won't spoil.

Incidentally, as of this writing, it's been selling pretty steadily for $1.40 a pound at one of our local natural-food stores. (Bring your own container!)

Chocolate is one of the most universally beloved flavors of all time. How unfortunate that it's so unhealthy! It's full of oxalic acid, which prevents the body from absorbing calcium. It contains caffeine and other harmful substances. Because of its bitterness large amounts of sugar must be used along with it. Many people are even allergic to it.

Luckily we have an alternative in carob, a food which tastes very much like chocolate, but has none of its bad qualities. In fact, carob has over twice as much calcium as chocolate, with only half as many calories and 1 percent as much fat. It contains 26 percent natural sugar and a generous amount of vitamins and minerals. Try some of the following recipes. You may get hooked on carob and find it easy to ignore the next candy counter you pass. Oh, and check the price... carob powder in bulk at natural-food stores is $1.25 a pound; cocoa powder at the local supermarket is $1.60, plus the cost of the additional sweetener it requires.

Carob Energy Balls

$^1/_2$ cup each carob powder, honey, peanut butter, sunflower seeds, and sesame seeds
$^1/_4$ cup each wheat germ and sifted soy flour
$^1/_2$ cup chopped peanuts or shredded unsweetened coconut

Combine the carob powder and honey in the top of a double boiler and cook them over hot water for a few minutes. Remove from the heat and blend in the rest of the ingredients, adding a few tablespoons of cold water if needed. Roll the dough into balls and coat them with the peanuts or coconut. Makes 20-25 balls.

Carob Pudding

$^1/_3$ cup sifted carob powder
$^1/_2$ cup boiling water
3 tablespoons cornstarch or arrowroot

1 cup skim-milk powder
2^1/2 cups cold water
^{1}/3 cup honey
3 egg yolks
1 teaspoon vanilla

Blend the carob powder and boiling water. Add the cornstarch, skim- milk powder, cold water, and honey, and blend until smooth. Pour the mixture into the top of a double boiler and cook it over boiling water, being careful not to let the water touch the top pan. Stir until the pudding thickens.

Beat the egg yolks, add some of the hot mixture to them, and pour it back into the pan. Continue cooking it over hot water for about 3 minutes more, stirring constantly. Remove it from the heat and stir in the vanilla. Pour the pudding into a bowl to cool. You may serve it with a little cold milk poured over it, if you like. Serves 6.

Carob Brownies

^{1}/2 cup vegetable oil
^{1}/2 cup honey
2 eggs
1 teaspoon vanilla
^{1}/3 cup carob powder
1 cup whole-wheat pastry flour
1 teaspoon baking powder
^{2}/3 cup chopped walnuts

Blend the oil, honey, eggs, and vanilla; gradually add the dry ingredients, stirring the nuts in last. Pour the batter into a greased square pan and bake at 325° for 20 to 25 minutes. Cut into squares when cool.

Carob Waffles

2 egg yolks
2 cups milk
2 tablespoons honey
3 tablespoons oil
$1^2/3$ cups whole-wheat flour
2 teaspoons baking powder
$^1/3$ cup carob powder
$^1/2$ teaspoon salt
2 egg whites

Mix the liquid ingredients first; then fold in the dry ingredients. Beat the egg whites until stiff and fold them in gently. Bake on a hot greased waffle iron. Try these with homemade jam either for Sunday breakfast or for a company dessert. Makes about 6 waffles.

Our Favorite 99¢ A Meal Recipes

Ruth keeps a recipe file that could be called eclectic. Some date back to her grandmother, others were the result of our many adventures while gathering material for our writing tasks.

For example, if we ran out of money, which did happen on occasion, we would make the first recipe given below. It's low cost, tasty and healthful — a true 99¢-a-meal winner.

Spuds and Carrots

This is so simple and yet filling and tasty. Boil up equal amounts of peeled potatoes and fresh carrots. When tender, add chopped raw onion to your taste along with some of your favorite herbs — we suggest cumin, paprika and a splash of soy sauce. Mash furiously and serve hot with a sprinkle of olive oil.

Tabbouleh Salad

1 cup bulgar wheat
2 cups minced parsley
$^1/_2$ cup sliced green onions

$^1/_3$ cup minced fresh mint
$^1/_2$ cup lemon juice
$^1/_3$ cup olive oil
$^1/_2$ teaspoon lemon rind
sea salt, fresh ground pepper

Soak bulgar in cold water until tender. Drain, squeeze out water by hand and combine with all ingredients. Chill for two hours and serve garnished with lettuce and tomatoes.

Oven-Fried Chicken

Dip pieces of chicken in buttermilk and then shake in bag containing whole-wheat flour, cornmeal, thyme and oregano (dry leaves), chili powder, and Parmesan cheese. Place in foil-lined baking pan in which you have melted butter or added a little olive oil. Bake at 400° for 25 minutes. Turn pieces over and bake another 25 minutes.

Turkey Loaf

1 pound ground turkey
$^1/_2$ cup bread crumbs
$^1/_2$ cup chopped onions
2 cloves garlic, minced, or 1 teaspoon garlic powder
$^1/_2$ cup minced parsley
1 cup stewed tomatoes   diced tom, tom sauce
$^1/_2$ cup milk and 1 egg
pepper, thyme, sage, celery seed

Mix well and bake at 350° for 1 hour. Makes great picnic sandwiches.

White Bean Casserole

1 cup Great Northern beans, soaked overnight. Cook until tender with 1 clove garlic, and salt. Save liquid for vegetable soup later. Add meat bones saved in freezer, large chopped onion, chopped celery stalk, fresh chopped tomatoes, basil. Put all in casserole and bake 1 hour at 350° covered, then uncovered for 10 minutes. Serve with French sourdough bread and butter.

Water Crisped Tortilla Chips

One dozen tortillas. Dip each in water and drain. Stack and cut into 6 or 8 wedges. Spread out in single layer on sheet and bake at 500° for 4 minutes. Turn over and bake until browned. Salt if desired. Cool and store in airtight container. Great when served with fresh salsa or various dips.

Tamale Pie

$^1/_2$ pound natural ground beef
1 cup diced onions
3 cloves minced garlic
$^1/_4$ cup stock
2 tablespoons whole-wheat flour
2 tablespoons chili powder
$1^1/_2$ teaspoons cumin
$1^1/_2$ teaspoons crumbs
$^1/_4$ teaspoon cayenne
1 cup chopped tomatoes
1 cup corn
$^1/_2$ diced green pepper
$^1/_2$ cup tomato sauce
$^1/_2$ cup minced parsley
1 tablespoon fresh sage or $^1/_4$ tablespoon dry sage

Brown ground beef in oil. Add onions, garlic, stock and boil 5 minutes. Add flour stirring well. Add chili powder, cumin, crumbs, cayenne, chopped tomatoes, corn, green pepper, tomato sauce, parsley, and sage.

Crust:
1 cup cornmeal
1 cup cold water
2 cups stock
$^1/_4$ cup Parmesan cheese

Mix cornmeal with water. Add stock, cheese and cook for 15 minutes. Pour into 9x13 pan, add filling and top with Cheddar cheese and green pepper strips. Bake 30 minutes at 350°. Serve with crisp salad.

Salmon Loaf with Dill Sauce

16 ounce can salmon
2 eggs
1 cup crushed crackers or crumbs
$^1/_4$ cup chopped parsley
dried tarragon, thyme
1 tablespoon butter

Mix and bake 30 minutes at 300°. Drizzle butter on top and bake 3 minutes more. Serve with:

Dill Sauce

$^1/_4$ pound sweet butter
$^1/_4$ cup water
2 tablespoons fresh chopped dill (or dried)

Heat in saucepan. Pour over salmon loaf. Serve with baked potatoes and cucumber-tomato salad.

Stuffed Pepper Halves

3 large Bell peppers
2 cups cooked brown rice
$^1/_3$ cup sliced green onion
1 large tomato, chopped
$^1/_4$ cup chopped parsley
$1^1/_2$ cups grated cheddar cheese ($^1/_2$ cup on top)
2 eggs beaten
Worcestershire, basil, garlic, salt, to taste.

Cut peppers in half lengthwise, discard seeds. Drop in boiling water for 2 minutes. Then plunge in cold water. Mix ingredients and mound into peppers. Place in baking dish, sprinkle with cheese and bake 40 minutes at 375°. Great with hot sourdough bread.

Zucchini Bread

3 eggs
3 cups coarsely grated zucchini
1 cup oil
1 cup molasses
3 teaspoons vanilla
3 cups whole-wheat flour
1 teaspoon soda
3 tablespoons cinnamon
$^2/_3$ teaspoon nutmeg
$^1/_4$ teaspoon baking powder
1 cup chopped nuts

Beat eggs, oil, sugar, zucchini and vanilla. Mix flour and spices. Blend mixtures adding nuts last. Bake in two oiled loaf pans at 325° for 1¹/₂ hours. Cool 10 minutes and remove.

Zucchini Burgers

1¹/₂ pounds zucchini, shredded and squeezed
2 tablespoons butter
1 large onion, chopped and sautéed in butter
¹/₄ cup bread crumbs
2 eggs
¹/₄ cup Parmesan

Add all ingredients and form patties. Sauté in butter or olive oil until brown. Serve on toasted sesame buns with all the usual burger trimmings: sliced tomato, onion, lettuce, mayonnaise, mustard and ketchup.

Bran Muffins

¹/₃ cup oil
¹/₂ cup molasses
1 egg
1 cup buttermilk

Blend and add to:

1 cup whole wheat flour
1¹/₂ cups bran
1 teaspoon soda
1 cup raisins

Butter the muffin tins well before filling. Bake at 375° for 25 minutes.

Frittata
(Use large iron skillet for this)

³/₄ cup yogurt, half and half, or milk
6 eggs
2 tablespoons olive oil or butter
Parmesan cheese
¹/₂ green pepper, sliced
1 large onion, chopped
2 cloves garlic, sliced
1 cup sliced broccoli
1 cup sliced carrots

Sauté the above in oil until tender, then add the following in sufficient quantities to fill your pan about ³/₄ full: sliced zucchini, mushrooms, minced parsley, fresh basil, with pepper and salt to taste. Sauté some more until almost tender. Cover with beaten eggs-milk mixture, sprinkle with cheese. Bake at 375° for 20 to 25 minutes until eggs set. A crusty baguette with olive oil-balsamic vinegar dip would be tasty with this hot dish.

Potatoes and Bell Peppers ala Italiana

3 medium potatoes, sliced
1-2 bell peppers, sliced
1 onion, sliced
2 garlic cloves, minced
1 small can tomato sauce
2 tablespoons olive oil

Sauté potatoes, peppers, onion, garlic for 5 minutes in oil. Add sauce and cook over low heat for 35 minutes turning to keep potatoes from sticking. Add a salad and you have a fine dinner at very low cost. Can be readily expanded to accommodate guests.

Carrot Raisin Muffins

1 egg
$^1/_2$ cup milk
$^1/_4$ cup oil
1 cup grated carrots
$^1/_4$ teaspoon salt
$^1/_2$ teaspoon cinnamon
$^1/_2$ cup raisins
$1^1/_2$ cups whole-wheat pastry flour

Mix in order, adding flour last, and bake at 350° for 25 minutes in well-buttered muffin tins or paper shells.

Ruth's Almond Cookies

Grind about $^2/_3$ cup of almonds in blender. Mix with $^1/_4$ cup butter, $^1/_2$ cup honey, 1 teaspoon almond flavoring, $^1/_4$ cup wheat germ, $^2/_3$ cup whole-wheat pastry flour or enough to make soft batter. Spread in square pan and bake about 15 minutes at 350°. Cut into bars.

Epilog

It is vital to good health to consume a varied, natural diet that provides everything the body needs to maintain and repair itself. It is also essential to feed the mind with the spiritual food that it requires for optimum performance. Stated simply, your well-being depends on what you do as much or more as what you eat!

In a study by Donald Pelletier of Stanford, author of *Mind as Slayer, Mind as Healer*, he proved that about 80 percent of all illness is stress-induced. Further, Studs Terkel in his classic *Working*, described how most Americans dislike or even hate their jobs. If we combine these salient revelations with one from Nathan Pritikin, "McDonald's is doing a good job of killing America." It becomes clear why this country ranks so low on the world health scale.

Thus, to upgrade the value of this book, we'll include some related tips and pointers on lifestyles that will make the 99¢ a meal method more useful.

Wheels: Three million Americans live in trailers, campers and motor homes. It has become a delightful gypsy life with the opportunity to earn a living while you meander.

Boats: There are lots of liveaboard boats that need a bit of patching to make them a waterfront home. There are ways to do this that require no unusual knowledge or skill.

Microhouses: With a bit of land and one of these tiny dwellings you can wave goodbye to your landlord.

Gold: It's going up and now is an appropriate time to test out your talents as a prospector. It can become a profitable and enjoyable outdoor life.

Ranching for Free: There are many chances to leave the urban rat race and live as a gentleman farmer/rancher. What a great opportunity to grow your own organic food.

Hot Springs: There are nearly 2,000 and many are available as free campgrounds. What a fabulous place to vacation or LIVE!

Communes and Cooperatives: There are many with an open-door policy. Live a warm and friendly life with neat companions.

Cash in the Country: New high-tech communications systems allow anyone to enjoy the woods while taking a check from downtown.

Great Places to Just Hangout: There are thousands of unique and unusual locales for creative and innovative people.

The above have been well-researched and further information is available by writing the authors in care of Loompanics Unlimited, PO Box 1197, Port Townsend, WA 98368.

Information Sources

Books on Nutrition and Cooking

Blanchard, Marjorie. *The Sprouter's Cookbook: Fast Kitchen Crops.* Charlotte, VT: Garden Way Publishing, 1975

Brown, Edward E. *The Tassajara Bread Book.* Berkeley: Shambhala, 1970.

Brown, Edward E. *Tassajara Cooking.* Berkeley: Shambhala, 1973.

Brown, Edith & Sam. *Cooking Creatively with Natural Foods.* New York: Ballantine, 1973.

Castle, Coralie & Margaret Gin. *Country Cookery of Many Lands.* San Francisco: 101 Productions, 1975.

Davis, Adelle. *Let's Eat Right to Keep Fit.* Rev. Ed., New York: Harcourt, Brace, Jovanovich, 1970.

Duquette, Susan. *Sunburst Farm Family Cookbook.* Santa Barbara, CA: Woodbridge Press Publishing, 1976.

Elwood, Catharyn. *Feel Like a Million.* New York: Pocket Books.

Ewald, Ellen B. *Recipes for a Small Planet.* New York: Ballantine, 1973.

The Farm. *The Farm Vegetarian Cookbook.* Seattle, WA: Book Publishing Co., 1975.

Hannaford, K. *Cosmic Cookery.* Berkeley: Starmast Publications.

Hunter, Beatrice Trum. *The Natural Foods Cookbook*. New York: Pyramid, 1961.

Kloss, Jethro. *The Back To Eden Cookbook*. Santa Barbara, CA: Woodbridge Press Publishing, 1974.

Lappé, Frances M. *Diet for a Small Planet*. New York: Ballantine, 1971.

Lee Su Jan. *The Fine Art of Chinese Cooking*. New York: Gramercy Publishing Co.

Martinsen, Charlene S. *Cooking with Gourmet Grains*. Seattle, WA: Stone-Buhr Milling Co., 1971.

Richmond, Sonya. *International Vegetarian Cookery*. New York: Arco, 1965.

Shurtleff, William, and Akiko Aoyagi. *The Book of Tofu*. Soquel, CA: Autumn Press, 1975.

U.S. Department of Agriculture. *Handbook of the Nutritional Contents of Foods*.

White, Karen C. *The Complete Yogurt Cookbook*. Austin, TX: Troubadour Press, 1970.

Willet, Mo. *Vegetarian Gothic*. Harrisburg, PA: Stackpole, 1975.

Books on Obtaining Food

Angier, Bradford. *Feasting Free on Wild Edibles*. Harrisburg, PA: Stackpole, 1972.

Fernald, Merrit Lyndon, & Alfred Charles Kinsey. *Edible Wild Plants of Eastern North America*. Rev. By Reed C. Rollins. New York: Harper and Row, 1958.

Furlong, Marjorie & Virginia Pill. *Wild Edible Fruits and Berries*. Healdsburg, CA: Naturegraph, 1974.

Gibbons, Euell. *Beachcomber's Handbook*. New York: McKay, 1967.

Gibbons, Euell. *Stalking the Blue-Eyed Scallop*. New York: McKay, 1964.

Gibbons, Euell. *Stalking the Far Away Places*. New York. McKay, 1973.

Gibbons, Euell. *Stalking the Good Life*. New York: McKay, 1971.

Gibbons, Euell. *Stalking the Healthful Herbs*. New York: McKay, 1970.

Gibbons, Euell. *Stalking the Wild Asparagus*. New York: McKay, 1970.

Graves, Richard. *Bushcraft: A Serious Guide to Survival and Camping*. New York: Schocken, 1972.

Kaysing, Bill. *The Robin Hood Handbook*. New York: Links Books, 1972.

Kirk, Donald R. *Wild Edible Plants of the Western United States*. 2nd ed. Healdsburg, CA: Naturegraph, 1975.

Medsger, Oliver Perry. *Edible Wild Plants*. New York: MacMillan, 1972.

Neithammer, Carolyn. *American Indian Food and Lore*. New York: MacMillan, 1974.

Smith, Alexander H. *The Mushroom Hunter's Field Guide*. Ann Arbor: University of Michigan Press, 1963.

Squier, Tom. *The Wild and Free Cookbook*. Port Townsend, WA.: Loompanics Unlimited, 1996.

U.S. Government Printing Office. *Survival Training Edition, USAF Manual 64-3*. Washington, DC: USGPO

Periodicals

Bestways Magazine, 466 Foothill Blvd., La Cañada, CA 91011.

Better Nutrition, 25 West 4th St., New York, NY 10036.

Countryside Magazine, Route 1, Box 239, Waterloo, WI 53594. (A fine small-stock magazine.)

Let's Live, 444 North Larchmont Blvd., Los Angeles, CA 90004.

Mother Earth News, 49 East 21st, 11th Floor, New York, NY 10010.

Organic Gardening and Farming, Rodale Press, Emmaus, PA 18049.

Prevention, Rodale Press, Emmaus, PA 18049.

The Total You, 13272 Ventura Blvd., Studio City, CA 91604.

Other Sources

For information on raising quails, write to Marsh Farms, 14240 Brookhurst St., Garden Grove, CA 92648.

For information on raising goats, write to Jerry Belanger, Route 1, Box 239, Waterloo, WI 53594.

For a catalog of fishing equipment, write to Memphis Net and Twine Company, Box 8331, Memphis, TN 38108.

For information on fishing, write to the National Fisheries Education Center, National Marine Fisheries Service, 100 E. Ohio Street, Chicago, IL 60611.

Index

YOU WILL ALSO WANT TO READ:

☐ **14181 EAT WELL FOR 99¢ A MEAL,** *by Bill & Ruth Kaysing.* Want more energy, more robust, vigorous health? Then you must eat food that can impart these well-being characteristics and this book will be your faithful guide. As an important bonus, you will learn how to save lots of money and learn how to enjoy three homemade meals for a cost of less than one dollar per meal. The book will show you how to shop, how to stock your pantry, where to pick fresh foods for free, how to cook your 99¢ meals, what foods you can grow yourself, how to preserve your perishables, several recipes to get you started, and much, much more. *1996, 5½ x 8½, 204 pp, Illustrated, soft cover.* **$14.95.**

☐ **14178 THE WILD AND FREE COOKBOOK,** *by Tom Squier.* Why pay top dollar for grocery-store food, when you can dine at no cost by foraging and hunting? Wild game, free of steroids and additives found in commercial meat, is better for you, and many weeds and wild plants are more nutritious than the domestic fruits and vegetables found in the supermarket. Authored by a former special forces survival school instructor, this cookbook is chockfull of easy-to-read recipes. *1996, 7¼ x 11½, 306 pp, Illustrated, Indexed, soft cover.* **$19.95.**

☐ **14175 SELF-SUFFICIENCY GARDENING, Financial, Physical and Emotional Security from Your Own Backyard,** *by Martin P. Waterman.* A practical guide to organic gardening techniques that will enable anyone to grow vegetables, fruits, nuts, herbs, medicines, and other useful products, thereby increasing self-sufficiency and enhancing the quality of life. Includes sections on edible land-scaping, greenhouses, seed saving and propagation, preserving and storing crops, and much more including fact filled appendices. *1995, 8½ x 11, 128 pp, Illustrated, Indexed, soft cover.* **$13.95.**

☐ **14176 HOW TO DEVELOP A LOW-COST FAMILY FOOD-STORAGE SYSTEM,** *by Anita Evangelista.* If you're weary of spending a large percentage of your income on your family's food needs, then you should follow this amazing book's numerous tips on food-storage techniques. Slash your food bill by over fifty percent, and increase your self-sufficiency at the same time through alternative ways of obtaining, processing and storing foodstuffs. Includes methods of freezing, canning, smoking, jerking, drying, and many other food-preservation procedures. *1995, 5½ x 8½, 120 pp, Illustrated, Indexed, soft cover.* **$10.00.**

Loompanics Unlimited
PO Box 1197
Port Townsend, WA 98368

NIN96

Please send me the books I have checked above. I have enclosed $_____ which includes $4.95 for the shipping and handling of orders totaling $20.00. Please include $1.00 more for each additional $20.00 ordered. Washington residents include 7.9% sales tax.

Name _____

Address_____

City/State/Zip _____

VISA and MasterCard accepted. 1-800-380-2230 for credit card orders *only.*
9am to 4pm, PST, Monday thru Friday.